OPTION TRADING CRASH COURSE

A Step-by-step Beginner's Guide To Creating Your Passive Income With Easy And Effective Strategies

Warren Stanson

© Copyright 2020 by Warren Stanson

All rights reserved.

This document is geared towards providing exact and reliable information with regards to the topic and issue covered. The publication is sold with the idea that the publisher is not required to render accounting, officially permitted, or otherwise, qualified services. If advice is necessary, legal or professional, a practiced individual in the profession should be ordered.

- From a Declaration of Principles which was accepted and approved equally by a Committee of the American Bar Association and a Committee of Publishers and Associations.

In no way is it legal to reproduce, duplicate, or transmit any part of this document in either electronic means or in printed format. Recording of this publication is strictly prohibited and any storage of this document is not allowed unless with written permission from the publisher. All rights reserved.

The information provided herein is stated to be truthful and consistent, in that any liability, in terms of inattention or otherwise, by any usage or abuse of any policies, processes, or directions contained within is the solitary and utter responsibility of the recipient reader. Under no circumstances will any legal responsibility or blame be held against the publisher for any reparation, damages, or monetary loss due to the information herein, either directly or indirectly.

Respective authors own all copyrights not held by the publisher.

The information herein is offered for informational purposes solely, and is universal as so. The presentation of the information is without contract or any type of guarantee assurance.

The trademarks that are used are without any consent, and the publication of the trademark is without permission or backing by the trademark owner. All trademarks and brands within this book are for clarifying purposes only and are the owned by the owners themselves, not affiliated with this document

INDEX

INTRODUCTION VII

CHAPTER ONE 1

The ABC of Options Trading 1

    Unique Features of Options Trading 3

    Types of options contract 7

        Call option 8

        Put option 9

        How to calculate profit of options 10

    Option Writing: Selling an option contract 13

        How to calculate loss when an option is written 17

    Options vs. Stocks: Why you should trade options 19

        The profitability of trading options 19

        The many strategies of options 24

CHAPTER TWO 26

Price, Time, and Volatility: The Three Factors Affecting Trading Options 26

    Price 26

    Volatility 31

    The Four Option Greeks: Delta (Δ), Gamma (Γ), Theta (θ), and Vega (v) 38

        Delta (Δ) 39

        Gamma (Γ) 42

        Theta (θ) 43

        Vega (v) 45

Some minor options Greeks..46

Breakeven point: There is more to the profitability of an option 47

CHAPTER THREE 50
Strategies for Options Trading 50

Long Position Strategy (Call and Put) 51

Short Position Strategy (Call and Put) 52

Covered Calls and Protective Puts..54

Bull Spreads (Call and Put)...57

Bear Spreads (Call and Put) 63

Backspread (Call and Put) 68

Straddle (Long and Short) 73

Strangle (Long and Short) 77

Long Calendar Spread (Call and Put) 80

Diagonal Spreads (Call and Put) 84

Christmas Tree Spreads 88

Butterfly Spreads..94

Condor 96

Collar 99

Synthetic options 100

Risk Reversal.. 103

CHAPTER FOUR... 105
Options Trading Tips for Beginners 105

How to trade intelligently: The 3-2-1 Guide for Trading Options 109

Active learning..110

Calculative Planning 112
Seeking information 115
Discipline 118
Patience 119
Keep records 119
Having the right emotions and mindset for trading 120
Common mistakes to avoid during trading 127
Option trading platforms and tools 136

CHAPTER FIVE 141
Building a Trading Plan 141
Learn and Start 142
Study and Generate Ideas 143
Design and Build 145
Trade and Monitor 146
Exit and Record 147

CHAPTER SIX 149
Typical Days to Trade Options 149
Conclusion 152
References 154

INTRODUCTION

To attain financial freedom, you must make money work for you. This is one of the fundamental principles in the popular book, *The Richest Man in Babylon*. Money lying dormant cannot grow. And when it doesn't grow, you cannot attain the financial liberation you desire.

Investing money is the most veritable way to make your money grow — by working for you. Forms of investment include: cash, bonds, stocks, mutual funds, options, exchange traded funds (ETF), and alternative investments (e.g. commodities and real estate). With these investments, you legitimately multiply your money over a period of time.

One form of investment people seldom consider is options trading. Imagine this: Samsung releases a new smartphone into the market that goes for $800, and as a retailer and you decide to get 100 units to sell, but you don't have enough cash. You figure that by the time you'll get cash, the price would have risen to $1100. So you decide to place a bet. And here is how the bet works: you go to Samsung and tell them you predict that in three months the price of the phone would have increased to $1100. You reach an agreement with Samsung that if your bet is correct, you would be allowed to purchase the phone at $800. Samsung even gives you a sweeter deal — they tell you that your bet, if correct, would profit 100 units of the phone. That means, you would be allowed to purchase 100 units at $800 each, so you could sell at $1100. This is the basic way trading options works.

Trading options can be traced to 332 BC in ancient Greece, where a man called Thales bought the rights to buy olives prior to harvest. Since then options trading have been used in speculating market prices and amassing fortunes — from the tulip mania in 1636 to Jesse Livermore's bucket shops of the 1920s. Today, options trading has gone beyond olives and tulips; many corporate organizations — like Apple (AAPL), Facebook (FB), Disney (DIS), Netflix (NFLX), and others with active stocks — trade their stocks as options.

However, there are individuals who tend to shy away from trading options because of its apparent complexities. But this book will simplify these complexities and debunk the notion of options trading being a complicated form of investment. Just like every other form of investment, it only requires that you understand the nitty-gritty, which is why you have this book in your hands.

Options trading gives you the opportunity — the right — to invest in an asset which you do not own by speculating the future price of the asset. In simple terms, when you purchase an *options contract*, you have the *right* to buy or sell an asset at a particular price by a set date. Note: you aren't purchasing the asset directly, you are only purchasing the rights. This seems confusing a bit, but by the time you get to the last page, you will confidently educate a friend about options trading.

CHAPTER ONE

The ABC of Options Trading

There are many definitions to options trading. Optionseducation.org states that an option is a contract to sell or buy a specific financial product which is the option's underlying instrument or also known as the underlying interest. Cryptocurrency exchange company, *Binance* defines an options contract as an agreement that gives a trader the right to sell or buy assets at a predetermined price, either before or at a certain date. *Investopedia* says options are financial derivatives — that is, their value is reliant on an underlying security. The buyer of these derivatives have the right, but are not obligated, to buy or sell a security at a stated price and date.

These definitions all give three important information about an option:

—It is a contract; which means you are not purchasing the underlying asset directly, but a right to purchase.

OPTION TRADING CRASH COURSE

—It offers the buyer a right, not an obligation; which means you have the freewill to exercise this right or not.

—It is based on a fixed price and a fixed date.

These information make options trading different from other forms of investment. For instance, in stock trading, the investor buys or sells the direct stocks or shares of a company. An investor may buy 300 shares of a Silicon Valley company at $20 per share, study the market dynamics, sell these shares for $40, and make a 100 percent profit. But when it comes to options trading, this is not the case. With options, the investor is a forecaster, a speculator, a predictor. His playground is not the stock exchange, but the options exchange. At the options exchange, he predicts the price movement of an asset, and purchases the right to buy this asset at a certain amount on or before a certain date. Just as the name implies, he has the *option* to either exercise this right or not. So let's assume a Silicon Valley company has stocks that also trade as options, this investor may speculate that the stocks may rise from $20 to $40 by June 2020. Then he purchases an options contract for $10. In this contract he has the right to buy the stocks for $20 on or before June 30th. So if the stock rises to $40 on or before that date, he makes a profit, because while other investors are buying for $40, his option contract gives him the right to buy at $20; so he buys at this price and sells for $40. However, every investment has its risks, so his prediction may go south, and the price of the stock may plunge below $20. If this happens, he loses his principal.

This is a simple elucidation about what trading options entails, but there are unique characteristics about this investment method that makes it seem complex. However, we are going to explore its nuances step by step. By understanding the key features of trading options, you arm yourself with the skill and knowledge required to make your investment worthwhile.

Unique Features of Options Trading

The three unique features of options trading are: **strike price**, **expiration date**, and **options contract multiplier**.

Strike price: This is the fixed price at which the investor can buy or sell the security when the options contract is exercised. This is also called the exercise price. Going back to our example with the company at Silicon Valley, the strike price for the investor that purchased the $10 options contract is $20. That is if he exercises his contract on or before June 30th, he can purchase the security at $20, no matter how high the asset trades.

The strike price is the most important variable in options trading. It determines if the investor will be at a loss or profit. In fact, the investor makes speculations based on the strike price. Depending on the type of contract he purchases, he predicts if the security will have a value greater or lesser than the strike price. For instance, if his options contract gives him the right to buy a security at $20, then he would want the security to rise above $20. That way he can buy at $20 and sell at a higher price, say $40 and make a profit. But if on the other hand, the contract gives him the right to sell the security at $20, then he would want the security to go below $20. So he can buy at a lower price, say $10, and sell at $20.

Let's use another example to give a more lucid picture of strike price. Two investors, Smith and Mark, purchased options contracts to *buy* an asset on or before May 31st at a strike price of $50 and $70 respectively. Who will be in profit or loss if by May 31st the asset has a price of $60? Smith would exercise his right and buy the asset at $50, sell at $60, and make a $10 profit. However, for Mark, it is pointless buying at $70 only to make a loss of $10 if sold at $60, thus he doesn't exercise his option and it expires worthless.

But what if Smith and Mark purchased contracts to *sell* the asset on or before May 31st at a strike price of $50 and $70 respectively, and the asset trades at $60 by May 31st? Smith's option will expire worthless because it is pointless buying the asset at $60, sell for $50, and have a loss of $10. But this is not the case for Mark, because he can buy the asset at the current price of $60 and sell at his strike price of $70, to make a $10 profit.

Expiration date: This should be clear enough by now. It is the date after which the option cannot be exercised. Expiration date is what distinguishes the options trader from other traders or investors. The options trader works with time. His speculation is time-based. Other investors can forecast market price based on time, however, they are not constrained to buy or sell their stock at that time. For instance, in 2017 when the price of bitcoin hit close to $20000, there were traders who speculated this, however, when bitcoin hits this price, they didn't sell their bitcoin as they still hoped and speculated that the price may go higher. If this traders had options contracts, they would have sold (or bought) the asset because they know that if they didn't exercise their option on or before the expiration date, then it becomes worthless.

According to *Investopedia*, the expiration date for exercising options in the United States is usually the third Friday of the contract month or the month the contract expires. If Friday is a holiday, then the expiration date becomes the Thursday preceding the third Friday.

Options multiplier: From the details provided about options trading, we can see that there is a relationship between options contracts and stocks. Purchasing an options contract gives the investor the right to buy or sell stocks. But how much stock can an investor buy or sell when he purchases an options contract? This is where the multiplier steps in. The options contract multiplier provides the actual amount of shares the investor can buy or sell when the contract is purchased. The multiplier informs the investor on the actual size of the contract. As a rule, most options contracts are standardized at 100 shares, which means that 1 options contract equals 100 shares. So if Smith purchases an options contract of $7 per share, this implies that the actual worth of Smith's contract is $700. If this contract gives Smith the right to buy at a strike price of $50, it means that Smith would be able to buy $5000 worth of shares.

The good thing about the multiplier is that the investor can purchase more shares for a lower price as we will see later. Also, it gives a uniformity to the market, unlike in the stock market where there are no defined or standardized number of shares that can be purchased per time. This uniformity makes it easy to calculate the value of the contract. For instance if we are told that Smith purchased 4 contracts at $7 per share, we can do the math easily: 4 × $7 × 100 = $2,800. His total investment is $2800.

Now that we have explored the unique features that define options trading, we are going to see the types of options contract available.

Types of options contract

The definition of options contract tells us that a contract gives an investor or trader the rights to sell or buy an underlying asset. This implies that there are two types of options contract: the contract which gives one the right to buy or call shares to oneself (call option), and the contract which gives one the right to sell or put shares in the hands of another (put option). The market price of a call or put option is called a premium.

Call option

When you buy a call option, you have the right to buy an underlying asset at a strike price within an expiration date. Traders purchase calls when they expect the asset to have a value above the strike price within the expiration date. Call options are bought in a bullish market, that is, a market where the value of stocks keeps increasing. Theoretically, there is no limit to the profitability since the price of the stock can keep on increasing, since it is dependent on the demand (and supply) of the stock.

Let's go back to our previous example on Smith and John and include all the terminologies we have defined so far. Smith and John purchased call options each at $7 to buy shares at the strike prices of $50 and $70 respectively on or before the expiration date, May 31st. By May 31st, the price of the asset was $60, what does this mean for Smith and John?

First, they both purchased this contract at a total premium of $700. Recall that a contract (call or put) is worth 100 shares. So this implies that by May 31st, Smith has the right to buy 100 shares at $50 per share, and sell at $60. This gives him a profit of $6000 − $5000 = $1000. When you subtract the premium, that is the cost of his investment, Smith has a net profit of $300. However for John, his $700 investment expires worthless since the value of the asset is below his strike price. So while Smith gains $300 from a $700 investment, John loses $700.

Put option

This is the opposite of the call option. Purchasing a put option gives you the right to sell an underlying asset at a strike price within an expiration date. Investors buy a put option when they expect the value of the asset to depreciate below the strike price within the expiration period. Put options are bought in a bearish market — a market where the value of stocks keeps depreciating. The lower the decrease in value of the stock, the higher the profit made. However, in practice, there is the interplay between demand and supply which *supports* price movement and prevents the price from dipping further.

Assuming Smith and John bought put options at $7 at the strike prices of $50 and $70 respectively, this means that Smith would have the right to sell the shares at $50, while John would sell at $70. If by May 31st, the value of the stock was $60, what does this mean for these investors?

Remember their premium hasn't changed; it is still $700. So by May 31st, John can buy 100 shares at $60 and sell for $70, giving him a profit of $7000 - $6000 = $1000; subtracting his premium of $700, his net profit is $300. On the other hand, Smith's contract expires worthless since the stock value is above his strike price. Hence, he loses $700.

How to calculate profit of options

Calculating the profit or loss for options is quite different from stocks. The difference lies in the premium paid for options. When calculating profit or loss, it is not uncommon for new investors or traders to not take cognizance of the premium paid. They only consider the difference between the exercise price and current price of the underlying asset. Below are formulas to calculate profit/loss.

$$Profit_{direct\ stocks} = Selling\ price - Cost\ price$$

$$Percentage\ profit_{direct\ stocks} = \frac{Profit_{direct\ stocks}}{Cost\ price} \times 100$$

$$Profit_{call\ option} = (CMV - SP) - Premium$$

$$Percentage\ profit_{call\ option} = \frac{Profit_{call\ option}}{Premium} \times 100$$

$$Profit_{put\ option} = (SP - CMV) - Premium$$

$$Percentage\ profit_{put\ option} = \frac{Profit_{put\ option}}{Premium} \times 100$$

CMV = Current market value of stock, SP = Strike price

Let's see some examples.

—If Smith purchased 100 shares at $60 and sells them for $80, his profit will be: $8000 - $6000 = $2000. And the percentage profit will equal $2000/$6000 × 100 = 33.3%

—If he purchased a call option of $7 at an exercise price of $50, and the market value of the stock rose to $60, his profit will be: ($60 - $50) - $7 = $3. This means he makes a profit of $3 per share; so for 100 shares, his total profit is $300.

—If it was a $7 put option he purchased at a strike price of $70, and the market value of the stock dipped to $50, his profit will be: ($70 - $50) - $7 = $13. He makes a profit of $13 per share, thus having a total profit of $1300 for 100 shares.

There are no formulas for calculating losses for options purchased. This is because an option is either exercised or not exercised. If in a call option, the market value is above the strike price at expiry, the option is exercised and profit is made. At expiry, if the stock price falls below the strike price, the option is not exercised and it expires worthless. Thus, what is lost is only the premium paid. This is the same for a put option; if the option is not exercised because the current market value of the asset is above the strike price, the option expires worthless and what is lost is the initial premium.

For instance, if Smith didn't exercise his call option (or put option, since they have same price), he would only lose the premium of $700 (i.e. $7 × 100 shares) paid.

We calculate losses in options when option contracts are written (sold).

Key Points: Call buyer vs. Put buyer

Call buyer	Put buyer
• Has the right to buy stocks at a fixed price	• Has the right to sell stocks at a fixed price
• Profits when the market value of shares rises	• Profits when the market value of shares dips
• Speculates a bullish run	• Speculates a bearish run

Option Writing: Selling an option contract

So far we have only looked at options from the point of buying rights, however, these rights can also be sold. Selling an options contract (whether a call or put) is called writing an option. Options writing is slightly different from buying an option, because here, the seller has the *obligation* to deliver (selling a call) or buy (selling a put) the stock depending on its value at the time of expiration. Also, while a call option is bought when the market is bullish, it is sold in a bearish market; and while a put option is bought in a bearish market, it is sold when the market is bullish. Let's unfold this.

Smith buys a call option for $7 to be exercised on or before May 31st. If before, May 31st, he suspects that the price of the stock may dip, he may decide to sell this contract for $10 at an exercise price of say $60. What this means is: if the value of the stock rises to say $80, and the buyer exercises his right to buy, Smith has the *obligation* to buy the stocks at $80 and deliver them at $60 to the buyer. If this is the case, Smith would lose $1000, because he would have to deliver 100 shares at $60 ($6000), which he bought for $80 per share ($8000) — a difference of $2000; however, he got a $1000 premium ($10 × 100) from selling this option. Alternatively, if the value of the stock dips below $60 on or before May 31st, Smith keeps the entire premium of $1000 since the buyer of the option cannot exercise the right.

Another scenario: Smith buys a put option for $7 to be exercised on or before May 31st. He suspects that the price of the stock may rise before the expiration date, so he decides to sell this option. He writes a contract worth $10 with an exercise price of $60. This means that if the stock price dips to say $30 at expiration, and the buyer exercises his right to sell, Smith is obligated to buy the stock from the option owner at $60. He would have to hand out an extra $5000 to add to his premium of $1000 in order to purchase the stock. However, if the value of the stock rises above $60, he keeps the entire premium of $1000 as the buyer of the option cannot exercise his right to sell.

Recall that options trading is likened to placing a bet, but this time, the investor is reversing his initial prediction. An investor selling a call option is saying, "Yeah, I thought the value of the stocks would rise, but I think there would be a dip, so I am changing my position." On the other hand, the put writer is saying, "Well, the market value of the stocks would likely go up against my initial prediction."

This tells us that a call buyer and a put writer have same position — they predict an increase in market value of shares. While the put buyer and call writer have same position — they speculate a decrease in market value of shares.

Selling options contracts can be a high-risk venture. Since there is no limit to how high the price of an asset can increase, the writer of a call may record huge losses if the market price of the stock increases significantly above the exercise price. For instance, if, in our previous example, the price of the asset increases to say $150, Smith will lose $8000 — a loss that pales greatly in comparison to his $1000 premium. The only way he can circumvent this loss is if he already owned an equivalent amount of the shares in his portfolio before writing the call option. This is called writing a covered call. This strategy will be examined later in the book.

For selling put options, it is always better to sell put options of a security you want to own, that way it becomes an investment if the price of the security dips below the exercise price. For instance, if Smith wants to own this particular stock, purchasing it for $6000 because of the dip in price from $60 to $30 would only turn out to be a sort of investment for him. When the price increases at a future date, he can then sell. However, if he isn't interested in this security, then it becomes a loss for him.

It is not illogical to think that buying a call option is same as selling a put option, and buying a put option is same as selling a call option. However, the difference between any of the two cases lies in these two words: "right" and "obligation." The option buyer has the right to buy or sell the underlying asset, but the option seller is under the obligation to sell or buy the underlying asset. Let's explain it this way. Smith writes a call option for John. The market value of the asset rises above the strike price. John can decide to exercise his right by buying at the strike price, or he may choose not to exercise this right. If he exercises his right, Smith has *no option* but to sell the asset to him at the strike price. Smith doesn't have the right to decide not to sell.

The only similarity that exists between buying a call option and selling a put option, or buying a put option and selling a call option is the speculation of the parties involved. A call buyer and a put writer are bullish on the stock, while the put buyer and call writer are bearish on the stock.

How to calculate loss when an option is written

As you know by now, options writing is an inversion of options buying. The loss amassed when an option is *purchased* is only the initial premium paid. Conversely, the gain amassed when an option is *written* is only the premium received. Just like in our initial example where Smith keeps the $1000 premium if the option is not exercised by the buyer. However, if the option is exercised, he makes a loss. So how do we calculate losses?

$$Loss_{direct\ stocks} = Selling\ price - Cost\ price$$

$$Loss_{written\ call\ option} = (SP - CMV) + Premium$$

$$Loss_{written\ put\ option} = Total\ cost\ of\ shares\ at\ SP$$

CMV = Current market value of stock, SP = Strike price

Note: Losses always have negative value to indicate that the investor or trader is losing money.

Examples:

— If Smith purchased 100 shares at $60, and the value of the shares fell to $30, his loss will be: $3000 – $6000 = – $3000.

—But if he wrote a $10 call option at a strike price of $60, and the buyer exercised the option at a current market value of $80 at expiration, Smith will lose: ($60 – $80) + $10 = – $10. This is the loss per share. So for 100 shares, his total loss will be $1000.

—If it was a $10 put option he wrote at a strike price of $60, and the buyer exercised the option at a current market value of $30 at expiration, Smith's loss will equal the total cost of purchasing the shares at the strike price. In this case, he will lose $6000, that is, his $1000 premium and an additional $5000.

Key Points: Call buyer vs. Put buyer

Call writer	Put writer
• Profits from a decrease in value of shares	• Profits from an increase in value of shares
• Obligated to sell the shares at the strike price if the buyer exercises their right	• Obligated to buy the shares at the strike price if the buyer exercises their right
• Speculates a bearish run	• Speculates a bullish run

Options vs. Stocks: Why you should trade options

It is important to note that every form investment comes with a measure of risk. Some risks are higher than others. Therefore, it is expedient to carry out a comparative analysis to assess the risks of different investments. Just like every other investment, trading options is associated with risks. But let's explore the benefits of trading options and its comparative advantage over other forms of investment, especially stocks. We will examine these benefits under two rubrics: Profitability and Strategy.

The profitability of trading options

The profitability of trading options is three-pronged: (i) It is cost-efficient, that is, you use less to get more. (ii) It gives higher returns. (iii) It is less risky.

Cost-efficiency: It is cheaper to purchase an options contract than to purchase stocks directly. *Investopedia* quips that options have great *leveraging* power, so an investor can use a smaller investment to purchase an options contract which mimics a stock position. Let's explicate this with our investor, Smith.

Smith learns that Apple (AAPL) shares worth $50 per share. Smith wants to purchase 500 shares. There are two ways of doing this. He either purchases the shares directly from the stock market, or he purchases a call option contract worth $10 at a strike price of $50. How do we advise Smith on the best way to get these shares?

Let's look at how much Smith is going to invest if he purchases the stocks directly, and if he purchases options.

—Stocks:

To buy 500 shares at $50 per share, Smith would have to invest $25000.

—Options:

To get 500 shares, Smith would be required to purchase 5 call options contracts. Recall that 1 options contract is equivalent to 100 shares. Therefore, Smith's total investment will be 5 contracts × $10 (market value of the contract) × 100 shares per contract, which equals $5000.

This is how cost-efficient buying options is. Buying 5 options contracts will give Smith the same number of shares at a lower cost. Instead of spending $25000 buying the stocks directly, he spends only $5000, saving

$20000 which could be ploughed into another investment.

Higher returns: Options, when compared to other forms of investment, have percentage returns. Assuming the value of AAPL rises to $80 per share, Smith would make a profit of $40000 – $25000 = $15000. A 60% profit.

However, if he exercised his call option, he would buy the stocks at the exercise price of $50, and sell for $80, making a profit of $30 × 500 = $15000 minus his $5000 premium, which equals $10000. Analyzing this in cash alone, it may seem as though buying shares directly is a better investment, however when we calculate the percentage profit of the options contract, we would discover that this is not so. The percentage profit of the option = $10000/$5000 × 100 = 200%. So would you invest in stocks and get a 60% or buy an options contract and have a 200% gain?

Less risk: Due to its cost efficiency, trading options is a less risky investment than trading stocks. Let's go back to Smith to illustrate this.

If he had bought stocks, and assuming the price of the asset dips to $30, he would lose $25000 – $15000 = $10000. However, if on the other hand, he purchased 5 call options, and the price of the asset goes below the strike price of $50, his investment would expire worthless and he would lose only his investment of $5000.

Aside its cost-efficiency, options also minimize risks when used as a *hedge*. What is a hedge?

An investor, John, has 1000 shares of Alphabet stock (GOOGL). He is uncertain about the price movement of this asset; he suspects that in the future there would be an adverse price movement. So he makes another investment which would help mitigate his losses peradventure such adverse price movement happens. This new investment by John is called a hedge. A hedge can be explained as an investment which reduces the risk of drastic price movements of a security. It is like an insurance to mitigate loss in the future.

Investopedia states that the most common way of hedging is through derivatives. Recall that we defined options as financial derivatives — securities whose value are reliant on the value of an underlying asset. So how can options be used as a hedge to mitigate loss?

John purchased 100 shares of GOOGL at $15 per share. He then decided to hedge this investment by purchasing a put option worth $6 with an exercise price of $9 expiring in six months. Let's see what would happen to John's investment if: (i) he didn't hedge the investment and the value of GOOGL fell to $5, (ii) he exercised his put option, (iii) he didn't exercise his put option.

—Assuming John didn't hedge his investment, he would record a loss of $1500 − $500 = $1000.

—If he hedged his investment and purchased an option, he has the right to sell his stocks at $9 if the value of the stock goes below the strike price at expiration. So assuming the stock goes to $5, John can exercise his put option, and sell his shares at $9. That is, $9 × 100 = $900. His loss becomes $15 (cost of purchasing the shares) − $9 = $6. He loses $6 per share, or $600 for the 100 shares. This is a lesser loss when compared to the $1000 he would have lost if he didn't hedge the investment.

—Assuming the value of the stock rose above the strike price of $9 to say $18, John wouldn't exercise his option, and it would expire worthless. His only loss would be his total premium of $600. (Although if he hadn't hedged his investment, he would have made a gain of $1800 − $1500 = $300).

These three scenarios show how options act as a shield for investments. With options, the worst case scenario isn't drastic, as you are able to cut your losses instead of losing all your investment.

The many strategies of options

Excellent soccer coaches are those with the best strategies. They are coaches who are flexible and can adapt as the game changes. A good coach doesn't stick to one strategy or formation. Every game is treated differently. He studies his opponent and knows when to attack or defend, bearing in mind that he has just one goal: to win.

When it comes to investments, trading options is that good coach. In the real world, no market is ideal. Every market is affected by factors which control the demand and supply of an asset, and consequently its price. Due to these factors, the market is bound to fluctuate. However, trading options offers strategies that an investor can employ after considering past, current, and future market conditions. Ron Ianieri in an article for *Investopedia* noted that options trading is the only investment which offers diverse strategies to make profit in any market condition. And we are going to look at these strategies later in this book.

Thank you for reading my book till now. I'm sure you will enjoy the rest of it!

CHAPTER TWO

Price, Time, and Volatility: The Three Factors Affecting Trading Options

In chapter one, we looked at the basics of trading options. The examples we looked at were theoretical and "ideal". We used random figures in order to communicate these basics effectively. But this is not the case in practice. There is an interplay of factors that affect the price and profitability of options. These factors can be technical such as trends of price movement, or fundamental such as global news. But of the many factors that affect trading options, three stand out — price, time and volatility. These three are interlinked, and an investor's choice of trading options must be governed by them. They inform an investor's decision on how, why, and when to place a trade.

Price

Every activity in any market is centered on price. In trading options, we consider the price of the option (the premium), which is often controlled by the price of the underlying asset. The buyer of a call option would want the price of the asset to increase, while the buyer of a put option would want the price to decrease. The increase or decrease of the asset controls the value of the options contract. There are two value components of an options contract: Intrinsic value and Extrinsic value.

—An option's **intrinsic value** is the difference between the current market price of stock and the strike price of the option. For instance, if John purchased a $6 call option with a strike price of $44 for GOOGL currently trading at $48 per share. The intrinsic value of the option is $48 − $44 = $4. This means $4 out of the $6 premium is the intrinsic value of the option. The intrinsic value doesn't inform the trader about the profitability of the investment *per se*, it informs the trader about how the strike price favors the investment when compared with the current price of the stock. In options trading parlance: the intrinsic value tells the investor if he is "in the money," If he is "out of the money," or if he is "at the money." This is known as the moneyness of the contract. It is the relationship between the strike price of the contract and the current price of the asset.

$$Intrinsic\ Value_{call\ option} = Current\ price\ of\ asset - Strike\ price$$

$$Intrinsic\ Value_{put\ option} = Strike\ price - Current\ price\ of\ asset$$

—A call option is in-the-money or ITM if the current market value of stock is *above* the exercise price. The option is out-of-the-money or OTM if the current market value of stock is below the exercise price. And it is at the money (ATM) if the current market value of stock equals the exercise price.

—A put option is in-the-money when the current market value of stock is *below* the exercise price. It is out of the money if the current market value of stock is above the exercise price. And it is at the money if both current market value of stock and exercise price are equal.

—An option is near the money when the exercise price is close to the current market value of stock.

When the option is ITM, the investor has a higher probability of exercising the option at expiration.

There are two key points to note:

1. ITM options have higher premiums than OTM options. This is logical: the investor has a higher chance of profiting from an ITM option than an OTM option.

2. That an option is in the money doesn't mean it is profitable. The profitability of an option depends on the total cost incurred in purchasing the option (including the commissions associated with the option). Therefore, call option holders expect a very high movement in the price of the stock to cover the cost of the premium and, if possible, commissions. On the other hand, put option holders expect the price of the stock to drop for the same reason.

So in the above example, we can say that John is in the money because the current market value of the stock ($48) is higher than the strike price ($44) of his call option. However, if the current market value dips below the strike price, say $40, John would be out of the money. If the current market value moves to the strike price, John is at the money. On the other hand, if it were a put option with a strike price of $44, He would be ITM if the current value dips to $40, and out of the money if it increases to $48.

Normally, option writers would not want the intrinsic value of the option to be greater than the premium at the time of purchase. If this happens, the holder of the option can exercise it immediately and make excess profit. For instance if the underlying asset of John's $6 call option is trading at $54, the intrinsic value is $54 - $44 = $10. This is greater than the premium of $6; the additional $4 represents a profit for the option holder. Therefore, option writers prefer to sell options that have intrinsic value below the premium. However, as time progresses, the price of the asset may increase, and the intrinsic value may become higher than the premium.

—The **extrinsic value** of an option is the difference between the premium and the intrinsic value. Extrinsic value is the value contributed to the premium from other factors other than the price of the underlying asset. In other words, the value of a premium is composed of the value contributed by price of the asset (intrinsic value) and value contributed by other factors (extrinsic value). So for John's $6 call option with an intrinsic value of $4, the extrinsic value is $6 - $4 = $2. The extrinsic value of an option is determined by two basic factors: time and (implied) volatility.

Time

One of the fundamental characteristics of options is that they are time-bound. The expression, "time is of essence" hasn't been more appropriate elsewhere. As the time progresses, the value of an option decreases. This is why extrinsic value is also referred to as *time value*. An option contract with two months to expiration has more extrinsic value than an option with two weeks to expiration.

When there is more time until expiration, the option has a higher chance of becoming profitable due to a favorable shift in price of the security. For this reason, investors will pay higher premiums for an option that has more time until expiration than for an option with shorter time.

As a rule, an option loses 33.3% or one-third of its time value in the first half of its life, and loses the remaining 66.7% or two-thirds in the other half. The rate of decrease of time value as time progresses is known as *time decay* or *time-value decay*.

Volatility

Another parameter that affects the extrinsic value, and consequently the price of an option, is volatility. This is the fluctuation in price of the underlying asset. In other words, it is the rate at which the value of the asset moves up or down. Thus, an asset has low volatility if its price is relatively stable, while an asset whose price fluctuates easily (whether upward or downward) has a high volatility. In trading options, investors look at two types of volatility viz.: historical or statistical volatility (SV) and implied volatility (IV).

—Just as the name implies, *historical volatility* measures the price changes of the underlying asset over time. It is based on actual data, and can be measured over any period of time. High historical volatility signifies a greater change in price of the asset. Investors use historical volatility to predict future price changes of the underlying asset. This parameter informs investors on the speed of change in price, however it does not inform them of the direction. Let's illustrate this with a theoretical example by analyzing the historical volatility of two stocks, AAPL and GOOGL with a price of $70 and $90 respectively, in a one-week time period.

	Price ($)	
Day	AAPL	GOOGL
Sunday	70	90
Monday	72	90
Tuesday	71	90

Wednesday	70	90
Thursday	69	95
Friday	70	95
Saturday	72	100

From the table, we can see the fluctuation in prices. In this example, AAPL has a high historical volatility as the speed of change is high. On the other hand, GOOGL has a low speed of change, hence low historical volatility. One of the limitations of historical volatility is that it does not inform the investor on the direction of change. So in our example, the investor knows that AAPL dramatically changes, however he doesn't know that AAPL hasn't moved much from its initial price. On the other hand, he knows that GOOGL hasn't fluctuated much, but doesn't know that it is increasing steadily.

Usually, the higher the historical volatility, the higher the premium paid for the option. This is because an asset that fluctuates easily has a higher probability of being in the money at expiration.

Note: As a trader or investor, you don't need to bother calculating historical volatility yourself, there are several tools available that automatically gives the value as you trade.

Since historical volatility does not inform the investor of the direction of price movement, how does the investor predict the direction of price movement? This is where implied volatility comes in.

—With implied volatility, an investor predicts both the speed and direction of price movement. It is a more useful tool for investors than historical volatility as they can predict the future price of the asset as it trades. Usually the higher the implied volatility, the higher the price of the option; this is because an option is likely to be more profitable when there is a dramatic change in price of the asset. In historical volatility, investors use past trends to predict the price movement of an asset, however in implied volatility investors use factors such as company news, industry trends, and economic factors to predict the price of the asset. As a result, an options contract can have a high premium due to high implied volatility even when the stock price does not change.

For instance, let's say Facebook released a news that it would purchase TikTok. This news would lead to an increase in demand for Facebook shares, which would consequently increase the value of the shares. As a result, the premium of a Facebook option would also increase. However, there may also be a case where the price of the shares does not change because investors would want to see the effect of the new acquisition before making any investment. If this happens, the premium of the options would still increase even if the price of the asset remains the same. This is because the implied volatility would still be high as traders speculate an increase in value of the asset when the acquisition is made. Trading options revolves around predictions. Provided that there are factors that can back these predictions, the premium paid for an option may increase or decrease, even when there is no increase or decrease in value of the underlying asset. Take out predictions and the value of option contracts will fall. For example, if Facebook finally purchased TikTok, there would be no need to make predictions, and this would lead to a drop in implied volatility, and also the premiums on options written in that period.

Note: Implied volatility is founded on predictions, so there is a chance for the actual volatility to differ from what was predicted.

As an investor or trader who wants to buy or sell option contracts without necessarily trading the underlying asset, you must understand how implied volatility impacts premiums. The rule, just like in every other market, is to buy low and sell high. It may be investment suicide to buy an option with a high premium driven by implied volatility. When you see such an option, you should tell that there is a background factor that has driven its demand. Do your research before trading such option. The high implied volatility may be due to a company news such as an acquisition or merger, a new industry trend, or even an economic policy.

There are two fundamental points to consider about implied volatility: one, it is cyclical — a high implied volatility is followed by a low one, and the cycle continues; two, once the anticipated event happens, implied volatility falls. So an option purchased at an expensive premium due to volatility may yield losses. Therefore, it is best to consider selling options with high implied volatility, and buying those with low implied volatility. There are strategies for this, which we will treat in the next chapter.

Implied volatility plays a significant role in determining premiums. It also guides option buyers and writers.

Investopedia noted that listed options have a unique sensitivity to implied volatility changes. Short-dated options are less sensitive, while long-dated options are more sensitive to implied volatility. This is because short-dated options have lesser time to react to implied volatility, while long-dated ones have more time to react.

Strike prices are also sensitive to implied volatility. Strike prices which are near the money are more sensitive, while strike prices that are further ITM or OTM are less sensitive. This is also logical because the current market value of the stock has a greater propensity to increase above or below "near the money" strike prices than ITM or OTM strike prices.

The sensitivity of an option to implied volatility changes is determined by a parameter called Vega (v) — an option Greek.

The Four Option Greeks: Delta (Δ), Gamma (Γ), Theta (θ), and Vega (v)

As you know by now, the price of an option cannot be stable because it responds to various changes within the market. We have seen that it is sensitive to time and volatility. Asides these two, premiums are also sensitive to other measurable variables in the market, and the various sensitivities are measured with parameters called *Option Greeks*.

Option Greeks (or simply called Greeks) are indicators that measure the sensitivity of the price of an option to various market factors, and inform the trader about different risks associated with the trade. The Greeks are divided into first-order, second-order, and third-order Greeks. The commonest of all the Greeks are delta, gamma, theta, and vega.

First-order Greeks: Measure the change in the price of an option in relation to an influencing variable. They include Delta, Vega, Theta, Rho, Lambda, and Epsilon.

Second-order Greeks: Measure the change of first-order Greeks in relation to an influencing variable. They include Gamma, Vanna, Charm, Vomma, Veta, and Vera.

Third-order Greeks: Measure the change of second-order Greeks in relation to an influencing variable. They include Speed, Zomma, Color, and Ultima.

Delta (Δ)

This informs the investor about price risk. It measures or represents the change in price of an option for every $1 move in the value of the underlying stock. In simple terms, it represents how much money you will make or lose for every $1 move in value of the stock. For instance, if delta is 15, it means that you are going to make $15 if the stock moves up by $1, or lose $15 if the stock moves down by $1.

Call options have positive delta ranging from 0 to 1. This is because as the value of the underlying stock increases, the value of the call option increases. Conversely, put options have negative delta ranging from -1 to 0, because as the value of the underlying stock increases, the value of the put option decreases. The delta of call options approaches 1 as the value of the stock increases, and approaches 0 as it decreases. On the other hand, the delta of put options approaches 0 as the value of the stock increases, and approaches -1 as it increases. Let's see an example.

If John's $6 call option trading at $54 has a delta of 0.35, this means that as it moves from $54 to $55, John's option will worth $6.35. However, assuming it drops from $54 to $53, the value of John's option will be $5.65.

If it were a $6 put option trading at $54 with a delta of -0.35, John's option will worth $6.35 if the stock moves from $54 to $53, and worth $5.65 if the stock increased from $54 to $55.

Note: Beginners may tend to find the delta of put options confusing because of the negative value, however do not bother about it during calculation, the negative sign only indicates the inverse relationship (the direction) between the put option and underlying stock.

Furthermore, the value of delta depends on whether the option is ITM (profitable), ATM, or OTM (not profitable) as expiration approaches. The delta of ITM call options moves closer to 1 as expiration approaches, while that of OTM call options moves closer to 0 as expiration approaches. For ITM put options, their delta moves closer to -1 as expiration approaches, while OTM put options have their delta moving closer to 0 as expiration approaches. ATM call or put options have a delta of 0.5.

You could also think about delta in terms of probability. What is the probability of the option being exercised at expiration or expiring worthless? ITM call and put options have a higher probability of being exercised at expiration since they are profitable, hence their probability (or delta) approaches 1 (or -1 for put options). OTM call and put options have a lower probability of being exercised, so their delta approaches 0. ATM calls and puts have a 50 percent chance of being exercised or expiring worthless, thus they have a delta of 0.5.

Long-term options are less sensitive to price movement of the underlying asset, thus they have a low delta. Short-term options, on the other hand, are more sensitive to price movement of the underlying asset, and have a high delta. We can understand this either in terms of *risk* or *probability*.

In terms of risk, short-term options have higher risk than the long-term ones. If there is a dramatic change in price of the underlying asset, long-term options have more time to recover. But this is not the case for short-term options as they have lesser time to recover. It is like a marathon race: if in the final lap, a runner 5m to the finish line falls, he wouldn't have enough time to get up and win the race. However, assuming he fell 200m to the finish line, he still has a chance of winning the race.

Let's look at a hypothetical scenario. Smith purchased a call option with a strike price of $50 with 2 years to expiration. John purchased same option at same strike price but with 2 days to expiration. If the value of the stock falls to $48, Smith's call has more time to bounce back and become profitable, but not John's.

In terms of probability, short-term options have a higher probability of becoming profitable at expiration than long-term options. Going back to the marathon race, the runner 100m to the finish line in the final lap has a lower chance of winning than the runner who is 5m to the finish line. So in our previous example, if the stock increases to $52, John's call has a higher chance of profitability than Smith's call.

Gamma (Γ)

This measures the change of price risk. It measures delta's rate of change to a $1 change in price of the underlying asset. This is what we mean: We know that a $6 call option with a delta of 0.35 will become $6.35 if the price of stock moves from $54 to $55. But what if the price of stock moves from $55 to $56? What will be the new price of the option? We know that the price of the option cannot increase by 0.35 again. Reason: for a call option, the delta value increases as the price of the stock increases. So there must be a new delta value, and this is determined by gamma.

Gamma values are between 0 and 1. So if the $6 call option with a delta of 0.35 has a gamma of 0.15, the new delta will be 0.50. And the new price of the option increases from $6.35 to $6.85.

Gamma is usually at its highest (approaching 1) for NTM or ATM options, and lowest (approaching 0) for deep ITM or OTM options. This is because NTM or ATM options have more propensity to react to a change in price of stock. As a rule, long-term options have positive gamma, while short-term options have negative gamma.

Theta (θ)

This measures time risk. It informs the investor how much the option will lose value with each passing day. Options usually have a negative theta value because as the period of expiration draws close, the value of the option diminishes — everything being equal — as a result of time decay. This means that if the $6 call option has a theta of -0.70, it would lose 70 cents each day, every other factor being constant. With time decay, the option loses extrinsic value. This means long-term options have lower theta values than short-term options, since the latter are closer to expiration.

ATM options have higher theta than deep ITM or OTM options. We can explain this in two ways. Firstly, we can use extrinsic value or time value. Let's see this in the specific. In the 2011 Sci-Fi movie, *In Time*, time was the universal currency. Rich people hoarded enough time to make them immortal, while the poor hardly had more than 24 hours. Now let's relate this to the real world: If a thief wants to steal time, where would he likely go to? The home of the rich, right? And we know he would steal a whole lot of time. Peradventure he steals from the poor, what he would get would be so little.

This is how it is with options and time decay. The thief is time decay. The rich are ATM options. The poor are ITM or OTM options. The more time value you have, the more you have to lose. ATM options have zero intrinsic value and more time value. The more the time value in an option, the higher the time decay. Conversely, (deep) ITM or OTM have more intrinsic value than time value, so they experience low time decay.

The second way to explain why ATM options have higher theta than ITM or OTM options is to think of theta in terms of uncertainty of the option expiring worthless. We are 50 percent certain that an ATM option would expire worthless. However, if an option is deep in-the-money, we are almost certain that it wouldn't expire worthless — thus, our uncertainty is low. Likewise, if an option is deep out of the money, we are almost certain it would expire worthless. This means our level of uncertainty is also low.

Theta favors option writers, and is disadvantageous to option buyers. This is because as time progresses, the value of the option diminishes with a tendency of the option expiring worthless. However, if it expires worthless, this becomes a gain for the writer because they can keep the premium.

Vega (v)

This measures volatility risk. It measures how the option price would change with a 1% change in implied volatility of the underlying asset. We have already had an in-depth analysis of implied volatility. As the implied volatility increases, the premium of the option increases. So if a $6.35 call option has a vega of 0.05, and the implied volatility increases from 29% to 30%, the price of the option would increase to $6.40. While it would decrease to $6.30, if the implied volatility decreases from 29% to 28%.

Long-term options have a higher vega than short-term ones. This is because the former have a longer time to respond to volatility changes.

Some minor options Greeks

These minor Greeks are more detailed variables, and are often taken into cognizance by expert option traders.

—*Rho (ρ)*: Measures the change in option value with a 1% change in interest rate.

—*Lambda (λ)*: Measures the amount of leverage an option will provide in relation to a 1% change in the price of the stock. It is often expressed in percentage. For instance, an option with a lambda of 25 would have a 25% increase in the value being held in the option if the value of the underlying stock increases by 1%.

—Vomma: Measures the change of an option's vega in relation to the market's volatility.

—Ultima: Measures the change of vomma in relation to the market's volatility.

—Zomma: Measures the sensitivity of gamma to changes in implied volatility.

Breakeven point: There is more to the profitability of an option

In chapter one, we looked at how to calculate the profitability of options. We assumed an ideal market when making these calculations. However, since we now know that the value of an option depends on many factors — chief being price of underlying asset, time, and market's volatility — it implies that the profitability of an option is not a walk in the park. An option may be in-the-money at expiration, and yet wouldn't be profitable to the holder. An option holder can only make profit when the value of the underlying asset exceeds the breakeven point.

Breakeven point in options trading is the stock price that a security must reach for an option buyer to avoid a loss and make profit if they exercise the option. The breakeven point for call options is when the value of the stock equals the strike price plus the premium, while for put options, the breakeven point is when the value of the stock equals the strike price minus the premium.

This is a textbook definition of breakeven point. In practice, it is necessary to factor in all expenses, especially commissions, made toward purchasing the option. This means that for call options, breakeven point is when the value of the stock equals the strike price plus premium plus commissions. And for put options, the value of the stock equaling the strike price minus premium minus commissions is the breakeven point. However, for the purpose of clarity, we would stick with the textbook definitions in our examples.

$$Breakeven\ point_{call\ option} = Strike\ price + Premium$$

$$Breakeven\ point_{put\ option} = Strike\ price - Premium$$

John purchases a $7 call option with a strike price of $170. This means that for John to have profit, the stock should trade above $177. If it trades below this, say 173, John is in-the-money, but he wouldn't make any profit. If it trades at the breakeven point, John neither loses nor gains, he would only recover his premium.

If it were a $7 put option John purchased at a strike price of $165, he would profit only when the stock trades below (165 – 7) = $158. If it trades at say 160, John is in-the-money but has no profit. If it trades at the breakeven point, he only recovers his premium.

The breakeven point shows that making profit from an options trade goes beyond expecting the underlying asset to trade above or below the strike price. A $1 or $2 move in the value of the stock might be insignificant to a trader. A trader or investor would prefer to be *deep* in-the-money so that there will be extra left from his returns after recovering his premium and commissions. To ensure they make good use of the market and make huge profit, there are various trading strategies traders and investors adopt depending on the situation of the market.

CHAPTER THREE

Strategies for Options Trading

What makes options interesting is that it lives up to its name: it offers the investor or trader different *options* to choose from. Apart from giving an investor the option to buy or sell a security, options trading offers the investor diverse strategies for trading. It is crucial for investors and traders to understand and employ these strategies in order to minimize risks and maximize profits. These strategies confer on options trading a flexibility usually not seen in other forms of investment. Here is a list of the various strategies available:

1. Long position (Call and Put)
2. Short position (Call and Put)
3. Covered call and Protective/ Married put
4. Bull spread (Call and Put)
5. Bear spread (Call and Put)
6. Backspread (Call and Put)
7. Straddle (Long and Short)
8. Strangle (Long and Short)

9. Long Calendar Spread (Call and Put)

10. Diagonal Spread (Call and Put)

11. Christmas Tree Spread

12. Butterfly Spreads

13. Condor

14. Collar

15. Synthetic options

16. Risk Reversal

Long Position Strategy (Call and Put)

This is the basic strategy of trading options. In fact, all we have been explaining so far in this book is the long position. A long position (or simply called long) refers to when the investor buys an option expecting the underlying asset to increase or decrease in value. So an investor would hold a *long call* if they expect the underlying asset's price to increase, and hold a *long put* if they expect the price of the underlying asset to decrease. In both cases, the investor owns the underlying asset in their portfolio.

As you can deduce by now, the holder of a long call position envisages a bullish run, while the holder of a long put position expects a bearish run. The advantage of long positions is that holders can buy or sell at a locked-in price, and this helps to limit losses. However, holders of long options, especially long put options should tread with caution because it is possible for the price of the underlying asset to continue rising infinitesimally. If this happens, the investor loses their investment.

Short Position Strategy (Call and Put)

An investor taking a short position on an option does not own the underlying asset in their portfolio. With short positions, investors *write* an option — that is, sell — when they expect the value of the underlying asset to fall (short call) or rise (short put).

Short calls are high-risk investment undertaken only by expert traders who want to profit from a bearish market. As we saw earlier, the investor or trader is *obligated* to *sell* the underlying asset at the strike price if there is an increase in value of the asset, and the option holder exercises the option. Therefore, the investor can only profit if the option expires worthless. In this case, the maximum profit would be the premium received.

On the other hand, investors use the short put strategy when they speculate a bullish market. So they are *obligated* to *buy* the underlying asset at the strike price should there be a decrease in value of the asset. The good thing about short put options is that either way the market goes, the investor benefits. He always wins. If the underlying asset increases in price as he speculated, it expires worthless for the option holder, and the investor keeps the premium. However, if the underlying asset decreases in price, he is forced to buy the asset at the current market value from the option holder. What this means is that the investor has gotten the asset at a lower price than what he would have probably gotten it initially. He could *hold* this asset, wait till it increases in value, then sell.

Short positions are also called *naked calls* or *naked puts* because the investor does not have the underlying stock in his portfolio.

Note: When dealing with stocks, holding a long position on the stock means the investor has the stock in his portfolio and anticipates an increase in value. While holding a short position means the investor doesn't have the stock in his portfolio. He anticipates a decrease in value, so what he does is to borrow the shares from a broker, sell them at the current market price, and then when the price of the shares falls, he buys them back and returns them to the broker.

Covered Calls and Protective Puts

Covered. Protective. Two adjectives that have similar meaning. Any investor using this strategy squarely tries to shield himself from loss of the underlying asset.

Covered calls and protective puts are similar to short position strategies; the key difference is that the investor has the underlying asset. So he is not selling or buying an asset he doesn't already have. In a way, covered calls are a hybridization of long positions and short positions. Recall that in long positions the investor holds the stock, while in short positions, the investor does not hold the stock. So when an investor holds a long position for a stock, and decides to write an option against the stock, that option is covered.

In covered calls, the investor holds the underlying asset then writes a call option to give another investor or trader the right to buy the asset from him at the strike price. Unlike in short calls where the investor expects the price of the stock to decrease, writers of covered calls are normally neutral investors. They use this strategy when they do not expect the price of the stock to move significantly. So while they wait for a significant price movement, they write a covered call to make money from the premium.

For example, Smith bought 100 shares of GOOGL at $22 in December 2018. In July 2019, he then decided to write a $5 call option for the stock at a strike price of $26. Now if at expiration, the stock rises to $29, and the buyer of the option exercises their right, Smith is obligated to sell the stock at the strike price of $26. Smith doesn't lose anything because this is a covered call. His profit would be the premium of $5 received, plus the difference between the current market value of the stock and the price at which he bought it in December. So he gains a total of $9.

But if on the other hand the price of the stock drops to $19, the option expires worthless, and Smith loses $3. However, his premium mitigates his loss, and he retains $2.

The downside of covered calls is that the investor caps his profit, and doesn't benefit from a very significant increase in price of the stock. For instance, if the price of the stock had increased to $35 and no option was written, Smith would make $13 in profit. But since there is an option, he is obligated to sell at the strike price, and make a total profit of $9.

Protective puts are even more interesting for the investor. They insure the underlying assets of the investor. Protective put investors aren't neutral *per se*: they are actually bullish on the stock, but purchase a put option to *protect* against potential losses.

Whether a put option offers 100% protection depends on the moneyness of the contract. If the option is at-the-money, it offers a 100% protection until the contract expires. An out-of-the-money contract doesn't give 100% protection since the investor may likely lose part of his investment due to the fact that the strike price is below the current market value of stock. However, some investors who are willing to take some losses, purchase an OTM put option in order to cut down the premium.

For instance, Smith buys 100 shares of GOOGL at $50 and the stock increased to $60. But he doesn't sell because he feels that the stock may further increase in value. To hedge himself from potential losses and uncertainty as he waits, he decides to purchase a $3 put option with a strike price of $55. There are two possible scenarios that could happen at expiration.

One: The price of the stock may increase further. If this happens, he gains from the stock. Let's say the stock increases to $70, he would make a profit of $20. But since he purchased a put option (which expired worthless), his net profit would be $17.

Two: The price of the stock may fall below $55. If this is the case, he still profits from the trade but not as much as in the first scenario. For any price below the strike price, he would make a net profit of (55 – 50) – 3 = $2.

So protected put options are always a win-win for the investor. When an investor purchases the long stock and the put option at the same ratio and at the same time, such a protected put is called a *Married Put or Synthetic Long Call*. For instance, if Smith buys 300 shares of GOOGL at $50 on 31 March 2019, and on the same day purchased 3 put options at $3 each with a strike price of $55, Smith has a married put. If he had purchased only 1 put option, it is not a married put because 1 put option is not equivalent to 300 shares.

Bull Spreads (Call and Put)

Bull spreads are tricky. And risky. From its nomenclature — bull spread — we deduce that it is a strategy for expert investors and traders who anticipate a moderate increase in value of the underlying asset. In a bull call spread, the investor *buys* a call option of a lower strike price and *writes* a call of a higher strike price, with both options having the same expiration date. The range between the two strike prices is called the spread. As usual, the investor uses this strategy to limit his losses of owning the underlying asset, however it also has the downside of capping the profits made. Let's consider another example with Smith.

AAPL is currently trading at $40. Smith purchases a $9 call option for AAPL at a strike price of $50. Then he writes another option for AAPL at a premium of $2 and a strike price of $70. Let's consider what happens if AAPL trades at $80, $60, and $30.

Recall: For Smith to write an option, he expects the value of the underlying asset to decrease. If the asset increases and the buyer of the option exercises his right, Smith would have to sell the asset to him at the strike price. If the asset's value decreases, Smith keeps the premium as the option expires worthless.

—At $80, Smith would exercise his purchased option and make a net profit of (80 – 50) – 9 = $21.

However, he makes a loss with the written option as he loses $10 (that is, 70 − 80). But since he received a premium of $2, his net loss is $8.

This implies that Smith makes a $13 net profit from the entire investment. That is, profit from the purchased option plus loss from the written option. $21 + (−8) = $13.

—If AAPL trades at $60, Smith would exercise his purchased option and make a net profit of (60 − 50) − 9 = $1.

He also makes a profit from the written option by keeping the premium of $2 since the buyer of the option cannot exercise it.

So he makes a total profit of $3.

—If AAPL trades at $30, Smith's purchased option expires worthless and he loses the premium of $9 paid.

But he profits from the written option by keeping the premium of $2. Thus, the total loss on the entire investment is $7.

Note:

1. The premium of the purchased call is always higher than the premium of the written call. And

the difference between the two is the net premium.

2. Maximum profit in a bull call spread is made when the market value of the asset is above the two strike prices. It is calculated by the formula:

$$Maximum\ Profit_{bull\ call\ spread} = Strike\ price\ (written\ call) \\ - Strike\ price\ (purchased\ call) \\ - (Net\ premium)$$

3. Maximum loss in a bull call spread is made when the market value of the asset is below the two strike prices. And this is equal to the net premium.

Using the example above, we can see that the formulas hold.

Maximum Profit is made when the asset is at any price higher than $70. Therefore, maximum profit = 70 – 50 – 7 = $13. While maximum loss is made when the asset is at any price lower than $50. So, maximum loss = net premium = 9 – 2 = $7.

Bull put spread is the opposite of bull call spread. Here the investor uses two put options to create a spread and minimize the loss on his investment. Just like with calls, the investor purchases a put option with a lower strike price and writes a put option with a higher strike price, with both options having the same expiry date. Let's consider Smith and AAPL stocks.

AAPL is currently trading at $40. Smith purchases a $2 put option for AAPL at a strike price of $30. Then he writes another put option for AAPL at a premium of $9 and a strike price of $50. What happens if at expiration, AAPL trades at $80, $40, and $20?

Recall: Smith wrote a put option because he expects the value of the underlying asset to increase. A decrease below the strike price means that the holder of the put option exercises his right, and Smith is obligated to buy the stock at the strike price.

—So if the stock rises to $80, the purchased option expires worthless, and Smith loses the $2 premium.

On the other hand, the written put also expires worthless for the buyer, and Smith gets to keep the $9 premium.

This means that he has a net gain of $7 for his total investment.

—If the stock is at $40, the purchased option expires worthless, and he loses $2.

The buyer of the written option would exercise his right, and Smith would be obligated to buy the asset at the strike price of $50, and loses $10. That is, $50 strike price − $40 market value. However, this loss is cushioned by his $9 premium, so he only loses $1.

His net loss on the investment becomes $3.

—If the stock trades at $20, Smith would make a net profit of $8, that is ($30 strike price − $20 market value) − $2 premium.

For the written option, the holder of the option exercises his right, and Smith would have to buy the stock at $50. Doing this would lead to a $30 loss, which would be mitigated by his $9 premium, bringing his total loss on that trade to $21.

His net loss for the entire investment would be $13.

Note:

1. The premium of the purchased put is always lower than the premium of the written put. And the difference is the net premium.
2. Maximum profit is made in a bull put spread when the market value of the asset is above the two

strike prices. While maximum profit is equal to the net premium.

3. Maximum loss is made in a bull put spread when the market value of the asset is below the two strike prices, and it is calculated with the formula:

$$Maximum\ loss_{bull\ put\ spread} = Strike\ price\ (written\ put) \\ - Strike\ price\ (purchased\ put) - (Net\ premium)$$

So from our example, maximum profit is made when the asset is at any price higher than $50. At $80, Smith makes a maximum profit of $7. On the other hand, maximum loss is recorded when the asset trades at any price lower than $30. At $20, maximum loss = 50 − 30 − 7 = $13.

With bull spreads, there is a trade-off between making uncapped profits and minimizing losses.

Bear Spreads (Call and Put)

Just like the name suggests, the investor using this strategy anticipates a decline in the price of the underlying asset. This strategy is an opposite of bull spreads. Just like bull spread, this strategy helps the investor cap his losses, but it also limits profits.

In bear call spreads, the investor purchases a call option at a higher strike price and writes another call option at a lower strike price, with both options having the same expiry date.

Let's say AAPL is currently trading at $40. Smith purchases a $2 call option for AAPL at a strike price of $70. Then he writes another option for AAPL at a premium of $9 and a strike price of $50. Let's consider what happens if at expiration AAPL trades at $80, $60, and $20.

—At $80: Smith makes a profit of $10 (that is, 80 – 70) from the purchased option. However, because of the $2 premium, his net gain becomes $8.

For the written option, he loses $30 (that is, 80 – 50) as he has to sell the shares to the buyer at the strike price. But since he received a $9, his net loss will be $21.

The total loss on his investment becomes $13.

—At $60: Smith's purchased option expires worthless as the market value is below the strike price. The loss on that option is the premium paid, which is $2.

He loses $10 (60 – 50) for the written option since he has to buy the stock at the current market value and sell to the buyer of the option at the strike price. But the $9 premium received cushions this loss to $1.

This brings his total loss to $3.

—At $20: Smith's purchased option expires worthless and he loses only his $2 premium.

On the other hand, he keeps the $9 premium on the written option since it expired worthless for the buyer.

This gives him a total profit of $7.

Note:

1. The premium of the purchased call is always lower than the premium of the written call.

2. Maximum profit in a bear call spread is made when the market value of the asset is below the two strike prices. And it is equal to the net premium.

3. Maximum loss in a bear call spread is made when the market value of the asset is above the two strike prices. It is calculated with the formula:

$$Maximum\ loss_{bear\ call\ spread} \\ = Strike\ price\ (purchased\ call) \\ - Strike\ price\ (written\ call) - (Net\ premium)$$

Bear put spread is an inversion of bear call spread. Here, the investor purchases a put option with a higher strike price and writes another put option with a lower strike price, with both options having the same expiry date.

Let's assume AAPL is currently trading at $40. Smith purchases a $9 put option for AAPL at a strike price of $70. Then writes another option for AAPL at a premium of $2 and a strike price of $50. Let's consider what happens if at expiration AAPL trades at $80, $60, and $20.

—At $80: The purchased option expires worthless, and his loss is only the $9 premium.

The written option also expires worthless for the buyer, so Smith keeps the $2 premium.

His net loss on the investment becomes $7.

—At $60: He makes a profit of $10 (70 − 60) from the purchased option. But the premium reduces this profit to $1.

The written option expires worthless for the buyer, and Smith keeps the $2 premium.

His net profit on the investment becomes $3.

—At $20: Smith makes a profit of $50 (70 − 20) from the purchased option. However, the premium paid brings this profit to $41.

On the written option, Smith makes a $30 loss (50 − 20) because he has to purchase the stock at $20 from the buyer who exercised his option due to the depreciation in value of the underlying stock. But since he received a $2 premium, his net loss is $28.

Therefore, the net profit on the investment is $13.

Note:

1. The premium of the purchased put is always higher than that of the written put.

2. Maximum profit is made on a bear put spread when the market value of the stock is below the two strike prices. It is calculated with the formula:

$$Maximum\ profit_{bear\ put\ spread} = Strike\ price\ (purchased\ call) - Strike\ price\ (written\ call) - (Net\ premium)$$

3. Maximum loss is made on a bear put spread when the market value of the stock is above the two strike prices. And it is equal to the net premium.

Backspread (Call and Put)

A backspread is a complex strategy used only by expert traders. It involves the use of multiple options to accrue gains and limit losses. The key feature of this strategy is that the investor purchases more options (call or put) than he writes.

If an investor uses a call backspread or call ratio backspread, he would simultaneously purchase calls at higher strike prices and write calls at lower strike prices, with all calls having the same expiry date. As stated earlier, the number of written calls would be less than the number of purchased calls. The premiums from the written calls are used to purchase the new calls. *Investopedia* states that the most common ratios used in call backspreads are *one* ITM written call plus *two* OTM purchased calls, or *two* OTM written calls plus *three* ITM purchased calls.

This is a bullish strategy and the investor expects to profit from an increase in value of the underlying asset. It is mostly used when an investor or trader seeks to profit from increased volatility. For example, if a company announces a new product launch, investors may decide to purchase backspread calls. They anticipate an increase in the value of the asset, hence they purchased calls; however, to protect themselves from uncertainty and losses, they simultaneously write calls. For the investor to profit greatly, the value of the stock has to increase far above the strike prices. Let's see a hypothetical example.

GOOGL is currently trading at $30. John decides to execute a 2:1 call backspread by purchasing two call options at a $5 premium and strike price of $37. He then writes a call option for a premium of $7 with a strike price of $32. What scenario will play out for John if at expiration the stock trades at $50, $35, and $20?

—At $50: John exercises his two options, and makes a profit of $26. That is, 2 × (50 − 37). But the total cost of the two options purchased was $10, so his net profit becomes $16.

The buyer of John's written option would also exercise his option because the market value of the stock is above the $32 strike price. As a result, John loses $18 since he would have to buy the stock at $50 and sell at $32. But the $7 premium cuts this loss, bringing his net loss to $11.

This means that Smith makes a net profit of $5 from the call backspread.

—At $35: John's two purchased options expire worthless since the market value of the stock is lower than the strike price. His loss is the total premium of $10 paid.

John would make a little profit from his written option because of the premium received. When the buyer exercises the option, John loses $3, but since there was a $7 premium received, he makes a gain of $4.

However, his makes a total loss of $6 on the entire investment.

—At $20: John's purchased options expire worthless. And his loss is only the $10 premium paid for both options.

The written option also expires worthless for the buyer, and John gets to keep the $7 premium.

The total loss on the investment becomes $3.

As the market value increases far above the strike prices, the investor enjoys unlimited profits. But when the market value is very close to the strike price or below it, the investor suffers loss. However, this loss is cushioned by the premium received for the written option.

Just like call backspreads, put backspreads are a combination of put options in a certain ratio in order to maximize profit and mitigate loss. It involves buying put options with a lower strike price and writing put options with a higher strike price, with all puts having the same expiration date. Using this strategy, the investor anticipates a decrease in the value of the underlying asset. This strategy helps limit losses and makes profit limitless. *Investopedia* states that typical ratio of purchased puts to written puts is 2:1, 3:2, or 3:1.

If GOOGL is currently trading at $30, and John decides to execute a 2:1 put backspread, he may purchase two put options at a $5 premium and strike price of $32. He then writes a put option for a premium of $7 with a strike price of $37. What scenario would play out for John if at expiration the stock trades at $50, $35, and $20?

—At $50: The purchased put options would expire worthless. The loss on this trade would be the total premium of $10.

On the other hand, the written option also expires worthless, so John keeps the $7 premium.

This brings his net loss on the entire investment to $3.

—At $35: John's purchased puts would expire worthless, and the total premium of $10 would be his loss.

The buyer of the written option would exercise the option because the market value is below the strike price. As a result, John would lose $2. But since he received a $7 premium, he actually gains $5.

However, he has a loss of $5 on the entire investment.

—At $20: John would exercise his two put options, and make a profit of $24 (that is, $32 minus $20 multiplied by 2). But the total premium of $10 paid for the options brings his profit to $14.

The buyer of John's written option would also exercise the option, making John lose $17 (37 – 20). But since John received a $7 premium, his net loss become $10.

This means that he makes a net profit of $4 on the entire investment.

As the market value decreases far below the strike prices, the investor enjoys unlimited profits. But when the market value is very close to the strike price or above it, the investor suffers loss. However, this loss is cushioned by the premium received for the written option.

Straddle (Long and Short)

Investors or traders who use this strategy are often neutral about the projected price movement of the underlying asset. The investors expect a significant move in the price of the asset, but they are uncertain regarding the direction of the movement. So they combine two separate transactions so that the effect of one is neutralized by the other. Straddles are profitable when the value of the stock moves above or below the sum of the strike price and the premium.

Long straddle strategy involves *purchasing* a call option and a put option at the same time, strike price and expiration date. The strike price is usually at-the-money or close to it because investors aim to earn from a large price movement in either direction, which is usually triggered by a strong fundamental analysis such as news of an event.

A long straddle has uncapped profits and limited losses. However, using this strategy often comes at a high price. The investor isn't the only one anticipating the newsworthy event, the option writers also do. So they increase the price of the premiums such that it would cover part of their losses in a case where the option is exercised. Therefore, for the investor to profit greatly from the strategy, the price of the underlying asset must increase significantly over the breakeven point. Let's see an example.

Alibaba stock (BABA) is currently at $120. There is a rumor of Alibaba acquiring a film company in the US. Joan anticipates this event, however, she cannot accurately tell in what direction the price of BABA will move. So she purchases a call option at $5 with a strike price of $120, and also a put option at same premium and strike price. Both options have the same expiration. What would happen if at expiration BABA trades at $190, $110, and $50?

—At $190: For the call option, Joan makes a profit of (190 − 120 − 3) = $67

On the other hand, the put option expires worthless, and her only loss is the $3 premium.

Therefore, she makes a net profit of $64.

—At $110: The call option expires worthless, and the only loss is the $3 premium.

However, the put option is slightly in the money and Joan gains (120 − 110 − 3) = $7

This implies she makes a net profit of $4 from the entire investment.

—At $50: Joan loses only the $3 premium paid for the call option.

However, she makes a profit of (120 − 50 − 3) = $67 from the put option.

Therefore, her net profit from the entire investment is $64.

We see that the maximum loss that can be gotten with a long straddle is the net premium paid. And this only happens when both options are at-the-money at expiration. As long as the value of the stock is above or below the strike price, a loss in one option is offset by the profit in the other. However, for the investor to make maximum profit that would offset the total cost of the investment, the stock must trade very high or very low.

As deduced by now, a short straddle is an inversion of a long straddle. It involves the investor selling or writing a call and put option simultaneously at same strike price and expiry date. Unlike a long straddle, this strategy has limited profits and uncapped losses. This is why it is often used by expert traders when there is no significant movement in the price of the underlying asset.

Let's assume Joan wrote two options — a call and a put — for the BABA stock currently trading at $120. If the written options were worth $3 each and have a strike price of $120, what would be the outcome of Joan's investment if the stock trades at $190, $110, and $50?

—At $190: Joan loses $70 from the call option since she would have to sell the stock at the strike price of $120. However, the $3 premium received would reduce the loss to $67.

But she profits from the put option by keeping the $3 premium since the put would expire worthless for the buyer.

So she makes a net loss of $64.

—At $110: She makes a $3 profit by keeping the call premium which expires worthlessly for the buyer.

She makes a $10 loss on the put option since she has to buy the stock at $120 from the buyer. But the $3 premium reduces the loss to $7.

This means she makes a net loss of $4 on the entire investment.

—At $50: She makes a gain of $3 by keeping the call premium which expires worthless for the buyer.

But she loses $70 on the put option, which is reduced to $67 by the $3 premium.

This brings the total loss of the investment to $64.

Maximum profit can only be made when both options expire at the money, and the profit would be equal to the total premium received for both options. As long as the value of the stock is above or below the strike price, the investor would be at loss.

Strangle (Long and Short)

This strategy is similar to a straddle, but the difference is that the investor simultaneously buys or sells a call and a put option at *different* strike prices, but with the same expiration date. This is a neutral approach investors use when they anticipate a large price movement but are uncertain of the direction.

An investor holds a long strangle position when a call option is bought at a higher strike price while a put option is at a lower strike price, with both having the same expiration date. Profits are unlimited, while losses are capped.

Let's assume that Facebook (FB) is currently trading at $40, and Lisa decides to employ a long strangle strategy.

She purchases a $3 call with a strike price of $43, and a $2 put with a strike price of $37. What happens to Lisa's investment if FB trades at $50, $40, and $30 at expiration?

—At $50: She makes a profit of $7 on the call option, but the $3 premium reduces this profit to $4.

The put option expires worthless, and her loss is the $2 premium.

Her net profit is $2.

—At $40: Her call option expires worthless and her loss is the $3 premium.

The put option also expires worthless and she loses the $2 premium.

This brings her net loss to $5.

—At 30: Her call option expires worthless and her loss is the $3 premium.

But she makes a profit of $10 from the put, which becomes $8 when the $2 premium is factored in.

Her net profit for the entire investment becomes $5.

As long as the market value of the stock is between the two strike prices, the investor makes a maximum loss, which is equal to the net premium of both options. However, if the stock trades above the strike price of the call option, or below the strike price of the put option, the investor makes unlimited profit.

An investor holds a short strangle position when they write a call option at a higher strike price and write a put option at a lower strike price, with both having the same expiration date.

Facebook (FB) currently trades at $40, and Lisa decides to employ a short strangle strategy. She writes a $3 call with a strike price of $43, and a $2 put with a strike price of $37. What happens to Lisa's investment if FB trades at $50, $40, and $30 at expiration?

—At $50: She loses $7 from the call option since she would have to sell the shares at the strike price. But since she received a premium of $3, the loss is reduced to $4.

She profits from the put option since it expires worthless for the buyer and she gets to keep the $2 premium.

This makes the net loss on the entire investment $2.

—At $40: The call option expires worthless and she keeps the $3 premium.

The put option also expires worthless and she keeps the $2 premium.

Her net profit on the entire investment becomes $5.

—At $30: The call option expires worthless and she keeps the $3 premium.

Meanwhile, she loses $7 from the put option, but the $2 premium received reduces the loss to $5.

Her net loss on the entire investment becomes $2.

Maximum profit is made in a short strangle when the market value of the underlying asset is between the two strike prices. Once the value of the underlying is above the call strike price, or below the put strike price, the loss becomes unlimited.

Long Calendar Spread (Call and Put)

Calendar can be a metaphor for time. So this gives us an idea on what a calendar spread strategy is. With this strategy, the investor purchases a *long-term* option and writes a *short-term* option for the same stock and strike price. Long-term and short-term means that the options have different expiration date. The aim of using this strategy is to profit through time decay with the short-term option, while the longer-term option maintains or amasses value.

If the strategy involves two call options, it is a long calendar call spread. If it involves two put options, it is a long calendar put spread.

For instance, let's assume that AAPL is trading at $100 and Smith wants to employ a long calendar spread with call options. He purchases a $5 call option with a strike price of $120 expiring in August 2019, and writes a $2 call option at same strike price, but expires in February 2019. What happens to the investment if AAPL trades at $80 and $140 at expiration?

For simplicity, we would assume that there would be no price movement between February and August 2019.

—At $80: The February call expires worthless for the buyer and Smith keeps the $2 premium.

But the August call also expires worthless for Smith and his loss is the $5 premium paid.

His net loss for the investment becomes $3.

—At $140: Smith loses $20 from the February call since he would buy the stock at $140 and sell it at $120 to the buyer who exercised the option. But this loss is reduced to $18 because of the premium received.

On the other hand, Smith makes a profit of $20 from the August call. Factoring in the premium reduces this profit to $15.

This implies that he makes a net loss of $3 from the entire investment.

From the example above, we see that the *only* way to profit from this strategy is for the shorter-term call to expire worthless and for the longer-term call to be in-the-money at expiration. This is the condition for unlimited profit using the long calendar method. So let's assume that AAPL trades at $110 in February and rises to $140 in August. The February call expires worthless and Smith keeps the $2 premium. In August, he would make a net profit of $15 (Market price – Strike price – Premium). This brings his total profit to $17.

Investors or traders use this strategy when they are bullish on the stock. However, they write short-term calls to reduce the cost of entering the trade.

Let's invert the scenario and see what happens if AAPL trades at $80 and $140 at expiration and Smith employs a long calendar spread by purchasing a $5 put option with a strike price of $120 expiring in August 2019, and writing a $2 put option at same strike price, but expiring in February 2019.

Assuming there is no price movement between February and August.

—At $80: Smith loses $40 from the written option because the buyer would exercise the option at expiry. But the $2 premium brings this loss to $38.

He makes a net profit of $35 from his own put option, that is Strike price – Market price – Premium.

The net loss on the entire investment becomes $3.

—At $120: The written option expires worthless and Smith keeps the $2 premium.

His put option also expires worthless and his loss is the $5 premium.

So the loss on the entire investment is $7.

Just like the long calendar call spread, a long calendar put is only profitable when the short-term put expires worthless and the long-term put is in-the-money at expiration. A long calendar put is adopted when the investor is bearish on a stock.

Another form of calendar spread strategy is the short calendar spread. This strategy is not popular among investors. It involves a purchasing a short-term option and writing a long-term one. It is a riskier strategy than long calendar spread since the time works against the investor. Unless there is a dramatic move in price at or before the expiration, the investor risks losing the purchased option. He would have to wait and expect that the written option expires worthless, and if that doesn't happen he suffers additional losses. This is a strategy used by expert traders in a volatile market who anticipate a dramatic price movement in either direction.

Diagonal Spreads (Call and Put)

A diagonal spread strategy has all the features of a long calendar spread except that the options used have different strike prices. In long diagonal spread, the investor purchases a long-term option and sells a short-term option at the different strike prices. While for a short diagonal spread, the investor purchases a short-term option and sells a long-term option at different strike prices. The level of the strike prices depends on whether the options involved are calls or puts.

In long diagonal call spreads, the investor is bullish on the stock and buys the long-term call at a lower strike price and writes the short-term call at a higher strike price. In long diagonal put spreads, the investor is bearish and buys the long-term put at a higher strike price and writes the short-term put at a lower strike price.

In short diagonal call spreads, the investor is bearish and buys the short-term call at a higher strike price and sells the long-term call at a lower strike price. For short diagonal put spreads, the investor is bullish, and buys the short-term put at a lower strike price and sells the long-term put at a higher strike price.

Most times, investors do not use short diagonal spreads, so we are going to concentrate only on long diagonal spreads. In practice, what happens is that as each short-term call expires worthless, the investor writes another till the expiry date of his own purchased call. So let's go back to investor Smith.

It is January and AAPL is trading at $100. Smith believes that AAPL would rise in coming months, so he decides to use a long diagonal call spread. He purchases a $5 call option with a strike price of $100 expiring in May 2019, and writes a $2 call option with a $110 strike price which expires in February 2019. What happens to the investment assuming AAPL increases by $1 every month?

A $1 increase means that Smith would write three additional short-term calls at the same strike price (February, March, April, May) which would all expire worthlessly since AAPL price is below the $110 strike price. Smith keeps all the premiums of these short-term calls, and makes a total of $8.

By May, AAPL would trade at $104, and Smith would make a $4 dollar profit. But because of the $5 premium paid, this profit becomes a $1 loss. However, he makes a net profit of $7 from the entire investment.

If on the other hand, we assumed a $1 decrease every month, the short-term and long-term calls would expire worthless. It will make no sense for Smith to write additional calls because they would be so out-of-the-money, thus their premiums would be so low that it wouldn't make a huge significance to his investment. Therefore, in this case, he loses his net premium of $3.

Maximum profit (with premiums factored in) is made from this strategy when there is a steady rise in the price of the stock which could rise above the strike price of the purchased call but not that of the written calls. Maximum loss is equal to the net premium and this happens when the price of the stock depreciates far below the strike prices.

Now let's see what happens when Smith believes that the price of AAPL will depreciate in coming months.

In January, AAPL is trading at $100. Smith believes that the price of AAPL would decline in next few months, so he decides to use a long diagonal put spread. He buys a $5 put option with a strike price of $100 expiring in May 2019, and writes a $2 call option with a $90 strike price which expires in February 2019. What happens to the investment assuming AAPL decreases by $1 every month?

With a $1 decrease monthly, Smith would write three additional short-term puts at the same strike price (February, March, April, May) which would all expire worthlessly since AAPL price is above the $90 strike price. Smith keeps all the premiums of these short-term puts, and makes a total of $8.

By May, AAPL would trade at $96, and Smith would make a $4 dollar profit. But because of the $5 premium paid, this profit becomes a $1 loss. However, he makes a net profit of $7 from the entire investment.

If there is a $1 monthly increase in the price of AAPL, all puts would expire worthless, and Smith would lose $3, his net premium.

Maximum profit (with premiums factored in) is made from this strategy when there is a steady decrease in the price of the stock which should be only below the strike price of the purchased put but not that of the written puts. Maximum loss is equal to the net premium and this happens when the price of the stock appreciates far above the strike prices.

Christmas Tree Spreads

This is a complex and high-risk strategy only used by advanced traders. It is a three-legged strategy involving six options. The investor buys and sells six options (call or put) with different strike prices but same expiration dates. With its 1-3-2 structure, the investor glides from a neutral to a bullish position. If an option has different strike prices, 1, 2, 3, and 4, an investor using a Christmas tree spread would *buy one* option at strike price 1, skip strike price 2, *sell three* options at strike price 3, and *buy two* options at strike price 4. So for a Christmas tree call spread, the investor buys one call option, sells three call options, and buys two call options — with the strike prices ascending (from 1 to 4) in each stage. An example of this is an investor buying a call with an $85 strike price, then selling three calls with a strike price of $95, and finally buying two calls having a strike price of $100. For a put, the investor uses the same 1-3-2 step, but this time, the strike prices descend (from 4 to 1) in each stage. For example, an investor can buy a put with a $100 strike price, and sell three puts with a $90 strike price, and then buys two puts with a strike price of $85.

Christmas tree spreads can be either long or short. What we defined above is the long Christmas tree spread. For short Christmas tree spread, the investor writes more options than he buys. Short Christmas tree call is a bearish strategy, and involves selling an option at strike price 1, skipping strike price 2, buying three options at strike price 3, and selling two options at strike price 4. Conversely, short Christmas tree put is a bullish strategy, and the strike prices descend from 4 to 1.

An easy way to remember the difference between long and short Christmas tree spreads is this: long spreads are "buy-sell-buy", while short spreads are "sell-buy-sell".

If GOOGL is $85, Smith may decide to apply a long Christmas tree call spread by executing an 85/95/100 spread. Let's say he purchases the $85 strike price call for $7, writes 3 calls with a $95 strike price at $2 each, and buys 2 calls with strike price of $100 for $1 each, how much profit or loss would he make?

The total cost of this trade would be: $6 (total premium received for 3 written calls) − $9 (total premium paid for bought calls). So Smith has a debit of $3.

—If the stock trades below $85, all the calls expires worthless, and his loss would be the cost of the trade, $3.

—If the stock trades at $95, Smith makes a $10 profit from the first purchased call. The written options expire worthless for the buyers, so he keeps the premium. While the last purchased call also expires worthless. His net profit becomes the $10 − $3 (cost of the trade) = $7.

—If the stock trades at 105, Smith makes a $20 profit from the first call, loses a total of $30 from the written calls, and makes a total profit of $10 from the last purchased calls. He has a net gain/loss of $0. That is, 20 − 30 + 10 = 0. So his net loss from the entire investment is cost of the trade, $3.

Maximum profit is made in long Christmas tree call spread when the stock price is at the strike price of the written calls at expiration. The maximum profit is the difference between the lowest strike price and the strike price of the written calls. The net premium (i.e. the cost of the trade) is also factored in. Maximum loss in a Christmas tree spread is equal to the net premium. This happens when the stock price falls below the lowest strike price at expiration in which case all options expire worthless, or when the stock price is above the highest strike price at expiration in which case all options are in the money and the net value of the options become zero.

Let's imagine that GOOGL trades at $100, and Smith decides to apply a long Christmas tree put spread by executing a 100/90/85 spread. He purchases the $100 strike price put for $7, writes 3 puts with a $90 strike price at $2 each, and buys 2 puts with strike price of $85 for $1 each. What would be the outcome of his investment if the stock price is below or above or at the strike prices?

The net cost of the trade is $3.

—If the stock price is above $100, all the options expires worthless, and Smith would lose only the cost of the trade, $3.

—If the stock trades at $90, Smith would make a $10 profit from the first put. The written puts expire worthless for the buyers. And the third leg of his investment also expires worthless. He would make a net profit of $7, after subtracting the cost of the trade.

—If the stock trades below $80, Smith would make a $20 profit from the first put, lose a total of $30 from the written puts, and make a total profit of $10 from the third leg of the trade. His profit/loss will be 30 − 30 = 0. So his net loss equals the net cost of the trade, $3.

For a long Christmas tree put spread, maximum profit is made when the stock price is at the strike price of the written puts at expiration. And it is the difference between the highest strike price and the strike price of the written puts, with net premium factored in. Just like with calls, the maximum loss is equal to the net premium. It happens when the stock price is above the highest strike price at expiration in which case all options expire worthless, or when the stock price is below the lowest strike price at expiration, making all the puts in the money and bringing their net value to zero.

Maximum profit in short Christmas tree call spread is equal to the net premium. This happens when the stock price is below the lowest strike price at expiration in which case all options expire worthless, or when the stock price is above the highest strike price at expiration in which case all options are in the money and the net value of the options become zero. Maximum loss is realized when the stock price is at the strike price of the purchased calls at expiration. It is the difference between the lowest strike price and the strike price of the purchased calls, with the net premium (i.e. the cost of the trade) factored in.

For a short Christmas tree put spread, maximum profit is equal to the net premium. It happens when the stock price is above the highest strike price at expiration in which case all options expire worthless and the net premium is kept as income, or when the stock price is below the lowest strike price at expiration, making all the puts in the money and bringing their net value to zero. Maximum loss is made when the stock price is at the strike price of the purchased puts at expiration. And it is the difference between the highest strike price and the strike price of the purchased puts, with net premium factored in.

Butterfly Spreads

This strategy involves four options (calls or puts) with the same expiration date, but three different strike prices — a higher strike price, an ATM strike price, and a lower strike price. The higher and lower strike prices are equidistant from the ATM strike price. What this means is that assuming the ATM strike price is $100, if the lower strike price is $90, then the higher strike price must be $110; a $10 difference on both sides. There are different forms of butterfly spreads but they all have one common feature: four options. Butterfly spreads have a 1-2-1 structure and they can either be long or short, and can be used with call and put options.

A long butterfly spread is a "buy-sell-buy" strategy and involves buying one option with a lower strike price, writing two ATM options, and buying one option at a higher strike price. The conditions and calculations for maximum profit and loss for long butterfly call and put spreads are the same for maximum profit and loss for long Christmas tree call and put spreads.

A short butterfly spread is a "sell-buy-sell" strategy and involves selling one option with a lower strike price, buying two ATM options, and selling one option at a higher strike price. The conditions and calculations for maximum profit and loss for short butterfly call and put spreads are the same for maximum profit and loss for short Christmas tree call and put spreads.

Other forms of butterfly spread are (long) iron butterfly and reverse (or short) iron butterfly. These strategies have a 1-1-1-1 structure consisting of two call options and two put options. The options have three different strike prices, but expire at the same date.

The iron butterfly involves buying a put option with a lower strike price, writing an ATM put option, writing an ATM call option, and buying a call option with a higher strike price. It is a "buy-sell-sell-buy" strategy. Maximum profit is the net premium received and it is realized if the stock price is equal to the center strike price, that is, the strike price of the written options. Maximum loss is the difference between the strike price of the purchased call and the strike price of the written call, with net premium factored in. This is realized when the stock price is above the higher strike price (of the purchased call), or below the lower strike price (of the purchased put).

Just as its name implies, reverse iron butterfly is a switch of the iron butterfly. Here, the investor writes a put option with a lower strike price, buys an ATM put option, buys an ATM call option, and writes a call option with a higher strike price. It is a "sell-buy-buy-sell" strategy. Maximum profit is realized when the stock price is above the higher strike price (of the written call), or below the lower strike price (of the written put). This is the difference between the strike price of the purchased call and the strike price of the written call, with net premium factored in. Maximum loss is solely limited to the net premium received and it is realized when the stock price is directly equal to the center strike price, that is, the strike price of the purchased options.

Condor

The investor or trader who uses the condor strategy holds a neutral position on the stock and hopes to profit from a price movement in either direction at reduced risk. It is a four-part strategy with a 1-1-1-1 structure. The four options expire on the same date, but have different strike prices — 1, 2, 3, 4. Condors can either be long or short, and are used with either call or put options.

A long condor call or put spread involves buying a call or put with the lowest strike price (1), writing a call or put with the second lowest strike price (2), writing a call or put with the second highest strike price (3), and buying a call or put with the highest strike price (4). It is a "buy-sell-sell-buy" strategy.

Maximum profit is realized in a long condor call or put spread when the stock price is between the center strike prices (2 and 3) at expiration. It is the difference between the second lowest (or second highest for put) strike price and the lowest (or highest for put) strike price, with net premium factored in. For both calls and puts, maximum loss is limited to the net premium, and it occurs when the stock price is below the lowest strike price at expiration, or above the highest strike price at expiration.

A short condor call or put spread involves selling a call or put with the lowest strike price (1), buying a call or put with the second lowest strike price (2), buying a call or put with the second highest strike price (3), and selling a call or put with the highest strike price (4). It is a "sell-buy-buy-sell" strategy.

Maximum profit in a short condor call or put spread is limited to the net premium, and it occurs when the stock price is below the lowest strike price at expiration, or above the highest strike price at expiration. Maximum loss is realized when the stock price is between the center strike prices (2 and 3) at expiration. It is the difference between the second lowest (or second highest for put) strike price and the lowest (or highest for put) strike price, with net premium factored in.

Another variation of the condor spread is the iron condor. It involves combining two calls and two puts with four different strike prices, but all having the same expiration date. An investor using this strategy holds a neutral position on the stock. It involves buying an OTM put far below the stock price, selling an OTM or ATM put slightly below the stock price, selling an OTM or ATM call slightly above the stock price, and buying an OTM call far above the stock price. The options that are further OTM protect against a significant downward movement of the stock price (purchased put) or a significant upward movement of the stock price (purchased call). Since they are further OTM, their premiums are cheaper.

The maximum profit in this strategy is limited to the net premium. This is attained when the stock price at expiration is between the center strike prices, that is, the written call and put. Maximum loss, on the other hand, is realized when the stock price is above the strike price of the purchased call, or below the strike price of the purchased put. This is the difference between the strike price of the purchased call and the strike price of the written call, with the net premium factored in.

Collar

This is also known as a *hedge wrapper*. Investors that use this strategy *already own the underlying asset* in their portfolio and expect a bullish move in the long run. However, they adopt this strategy to protect them against losses and uncertainty in the short term. Collar is a combination of two strategies we have looked at earlier — protective or married put, and covered call. The investor purchases an OTM put option and writes an OTM call option. The put option protects against a significant downward movement in the price of the stock, while the premium from the written call compensates for the put option purchased.

The call and put should have the same expiration date and have equal number of contracts. That means, if one put option is purchased, then one call option should be written. Maximum profit is reached when the stock price is above the strike price of the (written) call option. This is the difference between the strike price of the call option and the cost price of the underlying asset, with net premium factored in. Maximum loss occurs when the stock price falls below the strike price of the (purchased) put option. It is the difference between the cost price of the underlying asset and the strike price of the put option, with net premium factored in.

Synthetic options

Synthetic positions mimic the profit and loss profile of an underlying asset using only options, or mimic the profit and loss profile of an option using a combination of options and underlying assets. This strategy is superior to other strategies because they are used to adjust an existing position on a trade as the market changes. The transactions involved are also few, thus it doesn't cost much to enter the trade. There are four major types of synthetic options: synthetic long call and put, and synthetic short call and put.

A synthetic long call uses an underlying asset and a put option to mimic the performance of a call option. It is the same as a protective put or married put.

An investor using a synthetic long put strategy uses an underlying asset and a call option to mimic the performance of a long put option. It is used by investors who are bearish on a stock. Since the investor anticipates a decline in the value of the underlying asset and wants to sell, he buys a call option to protect the investment in case of a significant upward movement in stock price. It serves as an insurance policy just like a protective put, as the investor is not really out to make profit but to preserve his capital.

With this strategy, maximum profit is uncapped and is realized if the value of the stock drops to zero. It is the difference between the selling price of the underlying asset and the current market value (which should be at 0 for maximum profit), with net premium factored in. Maximum loss is the premium paid, and it occurs when the stock price is equal to the strike price of the (purchased) call.

One feature of synthetic options is short selling the stock, which also means holding a short position on the stock — where the investor makes profit by selling shares he does not own.

Synthetic short call involves short selling the underlying asset and writing a put option. The investor writes the put because he expects an increase in the value of the asset. However, if he feels that his prediction is wrong, he short sells the underlying asset to cushion any loss. The maximum profit using this strategy is the premium received for the put. It is achieved when the stock price is below the strike price of the written put. On the other hand, maximum loss is unlimited and it occurs when the current market price of the underlying asset is above the selling price of the asset. It is the difference between the selling price of the asset and the current market value of the asset, with the premium factored in.

Synthetic short put involves buying the underlying asset and writing a call option. It is similar to a covered call. The maximum profit is the premium received for the call, and it happens when the price of the underlying asset is above the strike price of the written call. When this happens, the buyer of the call exercises his option, but the investor loses nothing as the cost price of holding the asset is below the strike price. However, maximum loss is unlimited. It is realized when the stock price is below the cost price of the underlying asset. Maximum loss is calculated as the difference between the cost price of the underlying asset and the current market value of the asset, with the premium factored in.

Risk Reversal

This strategy is used as a hedge, and is also known as protective collar. The investor uses call and put options to protect against unfavorable price movements of the underlying asset. It involves *buying a call* and *writing a put* with both options having the same expiration date. Investors can use this strategy when they are short selling the asset. If the asset increases in value, they make a loss from the short sale, however this loss is offset by the purchased call. If the asset decreases in value, they make a profit from the short sale, but only when the stock price is at the strike price of the written put. If the price of the underlying drops below the strike price, then the investor is obligated to buy (back) the underlying asset at the strike price.

In another scenario, the investor can hold a long position on the stock, and use a risk reversal to protect his position by *writing a call* and *buying a put*. If the stock price drops in price, the put increases in value and compensates the loss of the long position. If the stock price increases, the investor profits from his long position as long as the stock price doesn't exceed the price of the written call. If the stock price exceeds the strike price of the call, the investor would be obligated to buy the shares at the current stock price and sell them at the strike price.

CHAPTER FOUR

Options Trading Tips for Beginners

If you are reading this chapter now, it means you have taken an interesting ride through the world of options trading. We know you are wondering why you didn't know such attractive investment opportunity till now. Or maybe you've heard about it, but it seemed all complicated then. And now, all you want to do is dive headlong into the sea of options. Hey, relax. There are other lessons you need to know. We don't want you losing money.

There are guides you need to follow to ensure you are trading right. Options are easy and flexible, yet a little misstep can cost you a lot. So here are some tips to guide you:

—In trading options you are making predictions. It is like forecasting the weather: the forecaster observes the elements and tells whether it will rain or snow. But on some days these forecasts may be wrong. So there is always room for uncertainty. Your predictions aren't foolproof. Always know that the market can swing against your prediction. Don't trust your expectations so much that you place a huge bet on the trade. It is true that investments come with risks, but the goal is to avoid or minimize losses.

—Always remember that the value of options is tied to the underlying asset. And the stock market is a very volatile one. The value of the underlying asset is governed by demand and supply; it is never constant. Therefore, it is important you study the trends (historical volatility) before purchasing an option. Also learn to anticipate the news. There is a mantra for this: "Buy the rumor, sell the news." *Investopedia* stated an interesting fact: "Wall Street traders don't try to follow the news. They try to anticipate it." The reason for this is simple: news can increase or decrease the demand for an asset, thus making the value of the asset skyrocket or plummet.

News can either be bad or good. If it is bad the stock price falls. An example of bad news include a bad earnings report. Good news such as a merger/acquisition, new product release or good earnings report, increases the value of stock. So good traders don't wait for the news, they source for it before it is announced. They stay informed. For instance, an investor may have a hint that Microsoft will make a new acquisition, so he decides to purchase a call option because he knows that when the news drops, demand increases and then he makes profit. But if the same investor gets the rumor that there is a huge drop in the revenue of Facebook, he may decide to purchase a put option in order to profit from the price drop when the earnings report is published.

Furthermore, be conversant with global socioeconomic climate. Be aware of new or modified policies and how they affect a company. Do not take option positions without knowing everything going on around the stock. Stay informed always. This leads to the next point.

—Belong to a community. Do not trade alone. The financial world is a huge community often made up of smaller communities. In these communities, there are CEOS, investors, venture capitalists, entrepreneurs, and so on. All these people are interested in how stocks perform. Information circulate within these communities, and if you are a lone trader you would definitely miss out. You can only buy the rumor when you hear about it. And you can't hear a rumor when you are not within a community. Also, being part of a community gives you further insights concerning trading options. You get new ideas and perspectives that you may not have seen before.

Social media has made being part of a trading community easy. There are open and closed Facebook, WhatsApp, and Telegram groups were trading information and the performance of the market are shared. You can also follow trading or investment bigwigs on their social media platforms. These individuals usually share what they think about the market or a stock. In fact, rumors spring from them.

—The stock market or options market is not like a shopping mall. In a shopping mall, no one loses. The buyer pays for the products they need. The seller accepts money they also need. It is a win-win for both parties. But in the stock market or options market, a trader's loss is another's gain. This is a fundamental principle you need bear in mind as you trade. An option that is profitable to you is unprofitable to another trader. When you purchase a call option expecting the value of the stock to increase, the call writer is expecting the value to decrease. It is a game. A clash of expectations. And you must endeavor not to be on the losing side. Be smart with your investment. Trade intelligently.

How to trade intelligently: The 3-2-1 Guide for Trading Options

Trading options is like a sport. In this sport, you are the coach, while your options, money and underlying asset are the players. As a coach, you need to be actively involved in the trade from start to finish. To be able to trade options intelligently, there are qualities you need to have. We have divided these qualities into three groups, and tagged them "The 3-2-1 Guide for Trading Options Intelligently". There are three qualities you need before trading, two during trading, and one after trading.

Qualities need before trading

- Active learning
- Calculative planning
- Seeking Information

Qualities needed during trading

- Discipline
- Patience

Qualities needed after trading

- Keep records

Active learning

Although hackneyed, "learning never stops" is a true saying. As a beginner in the options market, you have to dedicate time to learning. Learn from others. Learn from your losses. Practice. Practice. Practice. Make mistakes. Learn. And try again. Understand why you made a loss, so you avoid next time. Manish Sahajwani in an *Investopedia* article noted that the difference between successful traders and average ones is that the former learn from their losses and implement their lessons in their trading strategies.

You have to understand that the market is dynamic. So be flexible. You have to be willing to unlearn, learn, and relearn. What worked yesterday may not work today. Studying the historical and implied volatility can only guide you to the possible behaviors of the market, they can't tell what would actually happen. You have to find this out on your own. While it is good to belong to a community, do not always follow the crowd. Study the market yourself and have your own strategy.

There are beginners who feel trading options is a chore. They want to earn, but they don't want to work. Such traders often pay others to trade for them. This is bad practice. Trading options is not a get-rich-quick scheme. Neither is it a Ponzi or MLM scheme. You have to be intentional and responsible for your investment. It is risky to allow another trade for you. Such a person is bound to take dicey trading decisions that may jeopardize your investment, since the direct cost of the trade isn't on them. You can pay others to teach you, but never pay them to trade for you. You will never grow if you do.

Also, ask questions. This is important. Don't allow anyone bully you. There are expert traders who find it difficult to transmit knowledge. They forget that they were once beginners. Such traders are quick to hush you when you ask questions. Most times, they prefer you pay them a commission so they can trade for you. Don't agree to this. If one expert trader doesn't answer your question, find another. You would certainly find a fellow that is interested in your growth as a trader or investor. But if you don't find such a fellow, then there are tons of online sources on the internet. One trader said he spent 12 hours on YouTube watching videos on trading.

Take your growth personally. No one will do it for you.

You are reading this book, so we know you are already taking your growth seriously. Cheers!

Calculative Planning

Be a strategist. Before entering a trade, plan. Don't trade randomly. Trades aren't like chocolates you crave. When you crave chocolate, it is easy to just step out to the mall and get some. Trades aren't cravings. Also you don't copy and paste trades. That investor Smith purchased a put option for AAPL doesn't mean you should do the same.

Trades are serious business. They require planning. When you plan, it gives you a sense of direction. You factor in every variable and decide what should be done based on that variable. The first step in your plan is to select a trading style: Do you want to be a *day trader*, a *swing trader*, or a *position trader*?

A day trader is an active trader who trades options several times in a day to make profits before the market closes. Since the trade is carried out daily, a day trader usually depends on technical analysis (e.g. historical volatility) to guide his trade. They have no time to anticipate the news. They trade the news hoping to make profits as the news spreads within the day and the demand for the stock increases or declines. To be a day trader you must understand the market terrain. It is a risky approach for trading options. Time works against you.

Therefore, it is necessary you have enough capital. By enough we mean, your capital should be sufficient to capitalize on price movements, yet so small that you can risk losing it. Day trading is like a full time career as you have to study the performance of the market as time goes by. It is an activity that requires high level of experience and discipline. To be a successful day trader, you have to keep your emotions in check (we will discuss this later). You need to be strategic and flexible. Have enough strategy in your arsenal to employ based on the performance of the market.

If you feel being a day trader is exhausting, you can opt for swing trading. As a swing trader, you buy or sell options with expiry dates that span few days or several weeks. A swing trader analyses trends and volatility just like a day trader, but this time they may be concerned with fundamental analysis like news. They anticipate the news. They study the stocks and try to predict its price movement within a couple of days or weeks, then they take a position. It is not as tedious as day trading, however you may miss out on long term bullish or bearish moves since you are trading short-term options.

The position trader is one who holds long positions on a stock. As a position trader, you trade options with long expiry dates spanning several months or years as you anticipate an increase or decrease in the value of the stock. They are not active traders and are unbothered about short-term price fluctuations. They rely on both technical analysis and fundamental analysis for their trade. They focus mainly on the rumors — and trade ahead of time. They look out for huge profits since they do not make many trades in a year. With position trading, it is easier to be flexible with strategies. Strategies such as synthetic options or risk reversal work effectively with position trading since it affords the trader enough time to adjust his trade based on the price movement of the stock.

We have synthesized the table below from information culled from Optiontradingpedia.com to highlight key characteristics of the three trading styles.

Day Trader	Swing Trader	Position Trader
Watches the market all day long	Cannot monitor the market	Understand the dynamics of trading options
Invests in all the needed hardware and software	Doesn't require the needed	Good mathematical and analytical skills

	hardware or software	
Highly experienced and disciplined	Little emotional control and discipline	Little appetite for risk
Enough capital to sustain losses	Don't have a lot of money to trade with	Enough capital to make significant profits
Highly skilled and knowledgeable in technical analysis	Background knowledge of technical and fundamental analysis	Do not make wide or highly speculative guesses

After you have chosen a trading style, then you have to select the strategy that suits the current market performance and also your trading style. And be flexible with your strategies.

Seeking information

Right information is a fundamental secret to successful trading. Information is gold. The two key information you need are fundamental analysis (FA) and technical analysis (TA). We have mentioned these terms a few times but haven't really defined them.

Traders or investors use fundamental analysis to measure the value of a stock based on intrinsic (company) or extrinsic (industry, economic or political) factors. Fundamental analysis is usually divided into quantitative and qualitative categories. Quantitative deals with the measurement of numbers: company's sales, profit, assets, cash flows, expenses, etc. Qualitative looks at factors like company management, competitive advantage, products, acquisitions, mergers industry and governmental policies. According to *Investopedia*, Warren Buffet, The Oracle of Omaha, is one of the most famous and successful fundamental analysts.

There are other traders or investors who criticize fundamental analysis because they believe that, as *Investopedia* puts it, "all the news about a company is already priced into the stock." They believe squarely that the price movement of a stock is determined only by its demand and supply, thus are more focused on analyzing trends. Such investors are technical analysts. In technical analysis, investors use historical patterns to determine the price of a security. They believe that trends are bound to repeat themselves. So while fundamental analysts use current and future parameters to predict the price movement of a security, technical analysts use past trends of a stock to predict price movement. Technical analysts do not anticipate or sell the news. Everything they need is within the charts. And they are guided by some indicators like chart patterns, oscillators, moving averages, and support and resistance levels.

Fundamental and technical analyses have their limitations. So it is best to combine both when trading. The drawbacks of one are countered by the pros of another. For instance, it is a no-brainer to know that history will not always repeat itself. Therefore, if you expect a price movement based on historical trends, it is important to note that this trend may be altered by a strong factor such as a change in industry policies or an event (e.g. pandemic) that is catastrophic to a company. Analyze and filter the information you receive, especially in fundamental analysis. Before you take a position based on a news, ensure it is realistic and capable enough to cause a dramatic movement in the price of the underlying asset.

Discipline

Let's imagine you have a box load of new designer clothes. It is Black Friday, and you hear Nordstrom is giving massive discounts on your favorite products. What would you do? There is a high probability that you will jump on the offer immediately, even when you know there are so many designer clothes in your closet. The truth is you are not disciplined about your finances. And such trait is disastrous when trading options.

In options trading, the fluctuating price movement of a stock can affect your discipline. This is the reason many traders make mistakes that cost them their investment. Day and swing traders are more prone to indiscipline because they are racing against time. When you are disciplined, you understand that the fundamental characteristic of the options market is its dynamism. This should make you unperturbed as price swings upward and downward.

This is why it is important to develop a trading plan. A trading plan helps you maintain focus and dampen the noise. It helps you draft your goals and strategies, anticipate the directions and psychology of market, and know what to do per time as the market changes.

Patience

This goes hand in hand with discipline. You must be tethered to patience. Being in a hurry to make profits may cost you greatly. Not every trade is for you. Study the market to know when to enter or exit a trade. Impatient traders follow the crowd. They want to enter every trade and profit from it. Their portfolio is filled with a myriad of options. This is not a quality of a good trader.

Also, sometimes, when you enter a trade, allow the market take its due course. As long you have done your research and have convinced yourself that it is the right trade, then you stand a high chance of winning the trade despite market fluctuations. Don't exit a trade quickly because you are skeptical about market swings.

Keep records

Never forget what worked, and what didn't. It is good to maintain records on your winning and losing trades. Study them. Know what you did that made you win or lose. This is how you build your strategy and also your trading style. When you maintain records, you arm yourself with three sources of information — fundamental analysis, technical analysis, and your independent analysis. These three work together to make you profit more than you lose. Records don't lie. They show you your past performance, and if you are honest with yourself, you will come to terms with your actions or inactions that affected your performance. In essence, keeping records is one of the best ways to keep your emotions in check.

Having the right emotions and mindset for trading

When it comes to emotions, there are two enemies of a successful trader: greed and fear. But before we discuss these emotions fully, let's delve into what emotions are.

Emotions are *involuntary* responses to internal or external stimulus. So basically, you don't choose your emotions. When you see a dog, you become afraid. When you receive a gift, you are happy. Our body processes sensory information from our sight, hearing, touch, smell, and taste in order to yield an emotion. It can also use our internal environment to process information from a memory or thought to yield an emotion. Since emotions are involuntary and unplanned, human beings would have become a chaotic species. But this is not so because there is a way to counter emotions. And this is through our feelings. Unlike emotions, feelings are *voluntary*. We choose them. Feelings are the reactions we choose after we have processed an emotion. So when you see a dog, you can choose not to feel afraid and stand, or allow fear make you run.

So how does this relate to you, an options trader?

As a trader, you are receiving sensory information always from your eyes and ears, and these information can produce fear or greed. For instance, you are bullish on a stock, so you decide to purchase a naked call. Few months to expiration, the value of the underlying asset begins to dwindle. You become afraid that you would lose your investment. Experienced traders who have also purchased same contract are relaxed. They tell you that they are quite certain the price of the asset will rise on or before expiration. But you are more driven by your emotions, so you exit the trade to cut your predicted losses with the option being at-the-money. At expiration, the price of the underlying asset bounces back, and increases by 50%. You become awash with regret, but there is nothing you can do anymore.

This is what fear does to a trader. The truth is every trader has been afraid at one point or another. Fear is a normal, human emotion. It is involuntary. But the difference between seasoned traders and amateur traders is that the former control fear *in lieu* of being controlled by fear. They have disciplined themselves to stick to their trading plan. They only exit a trade when they are sure it is the right thing to do.

Psychologically, fear can be advantageous because it informs you of a perceived threat and shows you why you need to take action. However, if we go by the popular meaning of fear, that is, False Evidence Appearing Real, we would discover that what we are scared of most times are empty threats. Just like the brief example above, the price of the asset was not crashing. The dwindling price was just the typical feature of a dynamic market.

Another emotion is greed. It has been the bane of many traders, especially those without a plan. For instance, you hear a rumor about a new product launch. The price of the asset is on a consistent upward movement. Traders who have held their stock for a long time begin to sell and make huge profits. You do not want to be left out, so you purchase a call option, hoping to profit from the bullish trend. But immediately you purchase the option, the market psychology reverses, and the asset begins to dump, and soon your option expires worthless.

When it comes to greed and trading, there are two types of traders: there are traders who want to buy into every trade with the aim of accumulating profits across all trades, then there are the foolhardy traders who invest so much into a trade because they want to make huge profits. Exhibiting such emotions is detrimental, and usually costs traders their entire investment.

Keeping a cool head is a vital requirement for trading. Trading is 95% calculation and logic and 5% intuition. This means you should trade more with your head than with your heart.

The first step to managing your emotions is to overcome cognitive bias. Sean Vosler in his *7 Figure Marketing Copy*, a copywriting and marketing guide, defined cognitive bias as an error in thinking, analyzing, remembering, or other cognitive process, due to holding onto one's inclinations and beliefs in spite of contrary information. In the book, he outlined more than 20 types of cognitive bias, but we would dwell on the ones that affect many traders.

- *Bandwagon effect*: This is what we saw in our last example. It is also called FOMO: Fear Of Missing Out. You are concerned that you are missing out on the trade that every other person is cashing out from. So you want to join the party, even if it costs you so much to join. When this happens, you are primarily controlling your investment and trade from your heart, not from your head.

To overcome the bandwagon effect, you need to understand that not every trade is for you. Every human is unique, and so is every trader. That everyone is purchasing or writing a particular option does not mean you should do the same. This is why the importance of having a trading plan cannot be overemphasized. Have a plan and stick to it.

- *Overconfidence*: No matter your experience in the world of options trading, always act like a learner. Remember you are making projections and predictions. The market does not answer to you, you answer to the market. So it is risky when you are overconfident on a trade; the trade may fail. It is true that there is a place for instincts while trading, but it is still safer to be logical than emotional.

- *Outcome bias*: Sometimes, this is progenitor of overconfidence. This is when you make your trading decisions based on an outcome instead of how the decision was made. In our earlier example, there is a probability that you bought the options when the stock price was high, and still made enough profit because of the steady rise in value of the underlying. But this doesn't mean that entering into a trade to join the bandwagon is a good practice. That it worked yesterday does not mean it would work today. Do not base the success or failure of a trade because of one event. Successful trading involves a holistic consideration of many variables.

After overcoming cognitive bias, you can use some tricks to make sure you are not lured by your emotions. One way to do this is never to look at your profit or loss while trading. It is also a form of cognitive bias known as the Ostrich Effect — ignoring negative information by hiding your head in the sand; just like an ostrich. Your profit and/or loss during a trade is a dangerous information you don't need. Profits may be counterproductive, as they make you feel invincible. You can get carried away by this sense of invincibility and begin to make mistakes like over-trading. On the other hand, losses discourage you and affects you mentality. You begin to get into different trades just to compensate for the losses. Losses aren't compensated by making more trades. What you need is to go back to your trading plan, ask yourself pertinent questions, and try out a different method next time.

When you trade money you can afford to lose, then your emotions wouldn't be so invested in the trade. When you are greedy and invest so much capital because you want a huge profit, you become afraid about losing. This is how greed and fear work as partners. So conquer greed to conquer fear.

Another thing you need to understand is that failure is a part of life and losses a part of trading. Experienced traders or investors know this truth, so what they try to do is to curtail the rate of loss and ensure they make more profit. Successful traders or investors aren't individuals who have not lost money (are there even such traders?). They are people who have a high win-loss ratio because they have mastered their emotions. They aim to make the right decisions always, and avoid trading mistakes.

Common mistakes to avoid during trading

We learn from our mistakes. There is no better teacher in life than experience. But what if we don't have to make mistakes because we have learnt from the mistakes from others? Isn't that better? This is why we are going to discuss common mistakes traders, especially beginners, make during trading, and how to avoid these mistakes. We know that learning from your own practice sticks more, but let this guide be your chaperone; that little voice in your head telling you what not to do. We tagged them "The Ten Commandments for Successful Trading." So you shall:

1. Have a trading plan
2. Not buy cheap options
3. Not get carried away by the leverage of options
4. Not play too safe
5. Not fail to close trade before expiration
6. Belong to a community
7. Not trade low volume options
8. Not cut your losses by doubling up
9. Have an exit plan

10. Not believe that the more complex strategy yields more reward

Mistake 1: No trading plan

Every productive venture in life begins with a plan. From building houses to going to school to starting a relationship to starting a business. It all starts with a plan. Defining where to start, what to do when you start, and where to end. Amateur traders often make the mistake of thinking the trading options is just a hobby, a game. The charts are fascinating. The red and green candlesticks are attractive from the computer. But those candlesticks represent the condition of your investment. Therefore, it is important to treat your trades as a business. And a business starts with a business plan. Your plan should define how much you are willing to risk, the strategy you would adopt, and your exit strategy. We will discuss extensively on how to build a trading plan.

Mistake 2: Buying cheap options

Many traders begin trading by buying OTM options with short expiration dates because they are cheap. The plan is to spend less to gain more. They forget that they do not control the market. As the expiration date draws closer, the probability of the option getting in the money becomes slimmer. Most times for that to happen, traders have to bank on a strong fundamental analysis — which may or may not happen. Traders who purchase cheap options are attracted by the low premiums that they forget to actually guide their predictions with right analyses. Basically, they are taking a gamble. One which they may likely lose.

It is better to purchase ATM or ITM options. True, they may be more expensive, but you stand a higher chance of making profits from such options.

Mistake 3: Getting carried away by the leverage of options

What makes options so attractive is the multiplier or leverage effect. Beginning traders are more focused on the huge profits that can be made that they forget one important life's principle: the bigger the reward, the bigger the risk. If the trade swings to your favor, you gain the same or even higher profits than another trader who holds similar position in the stock market. However, if the trade goes awry, your loss is heavier because buying options includes paying premiums and other commissions. The risks in options trading is even greater when you are writing options, especially call options. If the written option doesn't expire worthless, you would have to buy the stock at a higher price, and sell at the strike price to the buyer. And sometimes, the premium received for the option can't mitigate such a loss.

So hold a small position as a beginner. Do not buy or sell multiple option contracts because you are gunning for huge profits. It is better to make consistent, small profits than to risk making a huge profit at once, then end up losing your entire investment.

Mistake 4: Playing too safe

Many beginners are so scared of losing their investments that they stick only with purchasing long calls and long puts. While it is good to be safe, such a practice will be detrimental to your trading experience because you won't grow as a trader. The options market is a dynamic one, that is why there are many strategies that you can use to flow with the progress of the market. There are strategies for any condition of the market — upward price movement (e.g. long call), downward price movement (e.g. long put), increased volatility (e.g. straddle), decreased volatility (e.g. calendar spread), no price movement (e.g. short condor), or time decay (e.g. iron condor).

Study the market and test these strategies with little funds. When you have mastered them, you can use them in the future to cash out from the market no matter which direction it goes.

Mistake 5: Failing the close trade before expiration

This happens to emotional traders. An emotional may fail to close trade before expiration because he is in profit and wants to make more — greed. Or he is at loss and expects the price of the underlying to move dramatically so he can make profit — fear. At the end, they probably forget to close the trade and their entire option expires worthless since it wasn't exercised. Trading options is always a race against a time, and you should not make the mistake of losing your investment just because you want more. There will always be more trades. The market is not closing, so cut your losses or take your profits instead losing everything.

Mistake 6: Not belonging to a community

Many traders try to trade in isolation. They do this because they are trying to protect themselves from conflicting ideas. This reason is logical because in a rowdy market with many divergent views, one may tend to get confused. However, this does not downplay the importance of belonging to a community. As a trader you need to stay informed. And there are news you would not get by trading alone. You have to interact and hear the ideas of others. It is your duty to sift the information you receive. How do you do this? If an idea is not in line with your plan then discard it. The idea may be worthwhile for another, but may be risky for you. A trader may suggest an idea because he has enough funds he is willing to risk to try it out. It will be foolhardy to try it out too with your little funds.

So receive information and process them before using them as tools for trading. But don't make the mistake of being uninformed.

Mistake 7: Trading low volume options

Low volume options are illiquid. There are many ways to look at liquidity. One, liquidity refers to the ability to buy or sell an underlying asset quickly without a change in price. Two, it refers to the presence of active buyers and sellers at all times trading a particular stock or option. When there is a high presence of buyers and sellers, there is increased competition and the bid-ask spread of the option is low. Bid-ask spread shows the difference between how much a trader is willing to buy an option and how much a trader is willing to sell an option. With illiquid options, this spread is high. Three (which is most important for us), the liquidity of an option refers to how quickly it can be sold or converted to cash at the current market price.

This implies that writing illiquid options may not be profitable for you. This is because you may not be able to even sell it, or if you do you would sell at a discounted price below the market price or the price you were willing to sell. Usually OTM options are more illiquid than ATM or ITM options. Also, long-term options are more illiquid than short-term options.

Mistake 8: Cutting losses by doubling up

This is another result of trading with your emotions. There are traders who choose to double up instead of exiting a trade. By doubling up, we mean taking the same trade position even when the market flows in the opposite direction. For example, a trader purchases a call option and before expiration, the price of the underlying *steadily* moves below the strike price. Instead of the trader to exit the trade, he buys another call option at a lower strike price hoping for the stock price to bounce back to an upward movement. Such practice heightens the overall risk of the investment.

As a beginner, you have to avoid this. Remember that a trader cannot control the market, but a trader can control their emotions and decisions. It is best you exit the trade early and move on. Go back to your plan and know what to do next time.

Mistake 9: Not having an exit plan

Every building has exits. When writing a business plan, an exit plan is included. So your trading plan should have a defined exit strategy. Traders make mistakes like doubling up because they don't have an exit plan. They don't know what to do when the trade goes south. Some option writers are guilty of this as well. They write an option and lean onto hope — expecting the option to expire worthless. But this is bad practice. Before writing an option make sure you have enough funds to buy back (written put) or sell (written call) the underlying if the trade doesn't go your way. You should understand that you have no control over when the buyer of the contract would choose to exercise the option. The buyer may choose to exercise it before the expiration, and you are obligated to trade at the strike price. So be prepared.

Furthermore, having an exit plan is not restricted to cutting losses alone, you should also have an exit plan even if you are in profit. Set a mark for yourself. For instance, as a trader, you can decide to take only 10% profit in each trade. It doesn't matter to you whether the asset further increases in value. Setting such standards and keeping to them helps improve your discipline and strengthen your emotion.

Mistake 10: Believing that more complex strategies have better rewards

As humans, we tend to take big risks because we think big risks yield big rewards. We are often motivated by mantras such as "No pain, No gain" or "No guts, No glory". These mantras are true. But we would recommend you take bigger risks if that is the only option available. In the world of options there are many strategies available, and each offers their unique risks and rewards. There is no point going for an iron butterfly when you can easily use a covered call. Study the market terrain and employ the best strategy suitable for the market and also your portfolio.

Stick with what works for you. Live by the two popular rules of Warren Buffet. "Rule No.1: Never lose money.

Rule No. 2: Never forget rule No.1." So stick to strategies you trust. Strategies that will make you profit. *Only* use a complex strategy when *necessary*.

You have gotten useful tips about trading intelligently, controlling your emotions, and avoiding common mistakes. The next question is, where do you apply these tips? What platforms can you use to trade options? What tools are available for you?

Option trading platforms and tools

Stocks are traded in the stock market. And the stock market is made up of many exchanges across the world. There is the New York Stock Exchange (NYSE), NASDAQ, London Stock Exchange (LSE), Japan Stock Exchange (JPX), and so on. In like manner, options are traded in an options market having exchanges that provide a location and platform for the easy trade of option contracts. These exchanges are not as many as stock exchanges but they perform their roles efficiently. The six most popular exchanges are Chicago Board Options Exchange (CBOE), Boston Options Exchange, Montreal Stock Exchange, Eurex Exchange, NYSE Arca, and International Securities Exchange. These exchanges offer options derivatives for thousands of securities.

The Chicago Board Options Exchange, established in 1973, is the biggest options exchange in the world having an annual trading volume of over 1 billion contracts. It offers options on over 2000 companies and over 20 stock indices, including S&P 500, S&P 100, Dow Jones Industrial Average, NASDAQ-100 and NASDAQ-100 Trust.

Traders key electronically into the Chicago Board Options Exchange and other exchanges through various brokerage platforms. These platforms act as third parties linking buyers and sellers of options. Here are examples of such platforms and what they makes them unique.

1. *tastyworks*: This platform is built for frequent options traders. So if your style is day trading, this is your go-to platform. It is tagged by *Investopedia* the best platform for advanced traders and mobile options traders. A trader can have a minimum account balance of $0.00 on this platform. They charge a $1 commission to open an options trade and a $0 to close. A review by *Investopedia* states the platform is built for "making decisions and taking action". The platform is designed to help you evaluate liquidity, volatility and probability easily. The ease of the platform is the same for

both their desktop, mobile, and downloadable versions.

2. *E*TRADE*: *Investopedia* says it is the best platform for beginners. Just like tatsyworks, a trader can a $0.00 minimum balance. However, they charge a commission of 50 – 65 cents ($0.50 – 0.65) per contract depending on the trading volume. Its higher platform, Power E*Trade, has a unique Spectral Analysis tool which helps you visualize maximum profit and loss for a particular strategy, thereby helping you understand your risks. In addition, there is a paper trading tool which allows you test strategies using delayed data. This unique feature helps you simulate trading positions and view the possible outcomes.

3. *eOption*: *Investopedia* recommends this platform as the best for low-cost options trading. Just like the aforementioned platforms, a trader can have a minimum balance of $0.00. But there is a commission of 10 cents ($0.10) per contract, and $1.99 per leg. A leg refers to one part or component of a multi trading strategy. For instance, a calendar spread is a two-legged, a butterfly spread is three-legged, and a condor is

four-legged. So if you are using the eOption platform and you apply a condor, it means you would pay a total commission of $7.96.

4. *TradeStation*: This offers low cost trade. It also runs a $0.00 minimum balance and charges 50 cents ($0.50) per options contract. According stockbrokers.com, the platform has built-in tools like custom grouping for current positions, streaming real-time Greeks, and advanced position analysis.

5. *TD Ameritrade*: It is rated the best broker for options trading tools. For stockbrokers.com, TD Ameritrade's app, Thinkorswim offers an impressive array of tools with features such as virtual trading with fake money, charting social sentiment, replaying historical markets, conducting real-time stock scans, and performing advanced options analysis. It offers a $0.00 minimum deposit, and charges a commission of 65 cents ($0.65) per contract.

6. *Interactive Brokers*: Stockbrokers.com says it is the best for advanced traders. Its tools are designed for expert traders and include algo trading, options

strategy lab, volatility lab, risk navigator, market scanner, strategy builder, and portfolio builder. They charge a commission of 65 cents ($0.65) per options contract.

CHAPTER FIVE

Building a Trading Plan

In the previous chapter, we emphasized having a trading plan. This is a blueprint to guide all trades. Your plan keeps you in check and stops you from making bad trading decisions. It is important that as a beginner you start trading options by first developing a plan. This inculcates in you the discipline you need throughout your trading activity. You can modify this plan as you grow, but the basic principles guiding your plan should be intact.

A plan is always made of steps. So in building a trading plan you need to follow certain number of steps. These steps will mirror the 3-2-1 guide mentioned earlier. And they are:

1. Learn and Act
2. Study and Generate Ideas
3. Design and Build
4. Trade and Monitor
5. Exit and Record

Learn and Start

Learning is the fundamental step in options trading. And as we have mentioned earlier — it never stops. But don't just learn, you have to practice what you have learnt. To do this, you need to start trading. How do you start?

- Select an options broker. We mentioned six in the previous chapter. There are a lot of options brokers. So do your own research and select the one that suits your trading needs. You can also get guidance from other traders. They can let you into the pros and cons of different brokers. Before choosing an options brokers, consider the following:

    - Are they regulated?
    - Are they experienced?
    - What are their charges — deposits and commissions?
    - What tools do they offer?
    - How friendly is their user interface?

- Fund your account: After you have selected your options broker, you need to fund your account.

Funding your account is totally at your discretion. Remember to trade money you are willing to lose.

Study and Generate Ideas

You already know that it is important to belong to a community. So study by interacting with other traders. Get information about the market (fundamental analysis) and combine with the charts (technical analysis). Use the tools and evaluate the volatility, probability and liquidity of contracts. Evaluate the fundamental options Greeks. When you have done all these, generate ideas to formulate a strategy for your trade. This involves:

1. Choosing your trading style
2. Choosing the particular underlying asset. Here are ways to find the best stocks to invest in:

- Research: Search for stocks with proven records of success. Research for news or events around those stocks. Follow the company's administrators on their social media platforms and monitor the company's websites and platforms for press releases, white papers, etc. Check for upcoming events that could affect the price movements of the stock.

- Liquidity: We have already talked about this. Check the bid-ask spread for the liquidity profile of the asset.

- Historical data and trends: This gives insight into the volatility of a stock.

- Employ the Greeks: Options Greeks are useful tools to determine how the stock would move, and how a 1% change in the stock price can affect your entire investment.

3. Choosing the strike price: To do this, you need to figure out if you have enough tolerance for risks, and also your expected returns. Conservative traders usually go for ATM or ITM options, while other traders who are risk-tolerant go for OTM options. You have to weigh the risk-benefit ratio of the strike price you have chosen. ITM options have a higher chance of success than OTM options, however they are more expensive. OTM options, on the other hand, are cheap and can make huge percentage profit if the stock rises or drops further above or below the strike price, but the chances of this is really slim.

4. Choosing expiration date: This should be guided by your trading style. If you are day trader, you would go for options that have close expiration dates. Swing and position traders usually trade far-dated options. Also bear in mind time decay and extrinsic value.

5. Exploring possible trading strategies to use: Ask yourself the following:

    - How do I expect the underlying stock to perform in a couple of days, weeks, or months?

    - What strategies would work efficiently for trading the underlying stock?

    - Do these strategies fit my trading level?

    - How complex are these strategies?

    - What are the risk-reward profiles of these strategies?

Design and Build

After you have generated your ideas, you can now design and build your plan. In designing, you determine how much you want to invest in the trade. This should be done after you have calculated your possible breakeven point, profit and/or loss. If your broker offers simulation tools, you can use to them to evaluate the possible outcomes of the trade. After designing, build your plan.

- Determine the particular strategy or strategies you would employ.

- Determine if you want a long-term or short-term position on the options.

- Also determine if you would adjust your position at any point and the conditions for such your adjustments.

- Determine the suitable time to cut losses or take profits.

- Choose your exit strategy.

Trade and Monitor

After you have built your plan, place your trade. You can choose to place and regulate the order yourself, or you can make your broker do the work for you. When you place and monitor the order yourself, your positions are regulated manually. You watch the price movements continuously, waiting till it suits your profit (or loss) position or your exit plan.

But the monitoring can be automatically done by your broker when you place a market order. This instructs your broker to buy or sell the option at particular price determined by you. This method is used by swing traders or position traders who do not have the time to gaze at their computer or phone screens all day.

The most popular market order used is the stop order. This is used to protect a profit position or mitigate further losses in a trade if the stock price goes awry. The stop order commonly used is the stop loss. Here, you set a stop price, and when the stock trades downward to that price, the contract or security is sold. In options, the buy stop order is triggered when the *bid* price is at or above the stop price, or the option currently trades at the stop price, or above it. A sell stop order is trigged when the *ask* price is at the stop price or below it, or when the option currently trades at the stop price, or below it.

Exit and Record

You ensure you follow your exit plan. Try as much as possible to do this because defaulting on your exit plan once may become habitual with time. And the results are not always friendly for your trade. So control your emotions and exit your trade when it is time.

After exiting, record your trades. Most brokers have a history log for every trade performed, so keeping a track of your trading activities is easy. However, we would advise that you have your own records. The history from your broker contains only numbers and probably the strategy you used. But your record would contain why you made a trade, why you used a particular strategy, and what your expectations were. If you are a day trader, you can record all the trades you performed in the day. Record the underlying asset, the strike price, the expiration date, the strategy, and the profit or loss of each trade, then your net profit or loss. Doing this would help you keep track of your performance. You would be able to ask yourself why a trade succeeded or failed. That way, you would know and focus on what you did right, and modify or completely do away with wrong practices.

You can also use your records to do a monthly, quarterly, biannual, or annual appraisal of your performance. You are your own boss. Your trade is your business. So as companies take stock, take yours too. The goal is to be the trader who has a high winning percentage. Keeping records is not actually easy but it is definitely worth it. Because it is the best way to optimize your trading.

CHAPTER SIX

Typical Days to Trade Options

Just like every other corporate world, the activity of the stock market is regulated by timing. Typically, the stock market opens by 9.30am (Eastern Time) and closes by 4.00pm (Eastern Time). This is the same timing for trading options. Between these times, trades undulate between highs and lows. It is like vehicular traffic. There is high traffic in the mornings as people head to work. Traffic is reduced during the day, and peaks again at evening as people return home. This is how it is in the stock market. As volumes of stocks are bought and sold, the stock prices keep changing throughout the day. Thus, there are best times (hours, days, weeks, and months) to trade options. Since options are tied to stocks, the price movements in the stock market reflects also in the options market.

In the morning, within the first one hour, prices of stocks are usually high due to increased volatility. As the market opens, news and events released from the close of the previous day to the opening of the new day are factored in. So as a beginner, you should avoid trading during these hours. Some day traders usually make short profits during this period, but it takes a high level of experience and skill to pull off.

As the clock hits 11.30pm or 12 noon, volatility begins to drop as many traders pause trading during this time. During this period, traders are waiting for more news or events to drop. Stock prices are relatively stable, and a beginner can place a trade at this point. Also, if you are privy to an upcoming event that other traders are waiting for, this is the best time to take a position, since you may likely get a low cost contract.

By 2.00pm and 3.00pm, volatility increases as traders place trades to make profits before the closure of the day. You should be quick to finish up your trades because stock prices can easily reverse during these hours.

Knowing the best days to buy and sell options depends on the type of options you want to trade. Regular options offer an array of expiration dates to choose from. The options usually expire on the third Friday of the expiration month. Weekly options or weeklies expire within eight days, and expire on Fridays. Quarterly options or quarterlies have expiration dates for the nearest four quarters in a year, and also the last quarter of the following year. They don't expire on the third Friday of the expiration month, but on the last day of the month. Long-term Expiration Anticipation Securities (LEAPS) are usually far-dated and expire in January, but can have expiration dates spanning three years.

Since different options have different expiry dates, the best days to trade is at the discretion of the trader. But to choose the days accurately, you would have to consider the time value, volatility, and liquidity of the options.

Conclusion

The options trading world is an interesting one filled with rewards — and risks. Through this book, we have comprehensively showcased this world to you. So start practicing. Trading options can give you that financial liberation you seek. This should be your goal. However, don't let it blind you to the voice of logic and reasoning. Let there be an interplay between your instinct and reasoning.

In addition, do not invest money you cannot lose. This is the golden rule. What is the point of trading options if you keep losing money because of your emotions? You are not trading to lose, you are trading to win. So let this be your watchword. But if you lose, don't be discouraged. Just try again. Learn from your mistakes and don't repeat.

Also don't forget to join a community.

Finally, we have shown you a goldmine. Don't fail to share with others. As you become a pro, invest time and knowledge into teaching others. This is one way to diversify your experience.

Now, go make your money work for you.

WARREN STANSON

It means a lot to me that you chose to read the book until the end. Thank you so much. Your feedback is truly appreciated: I would love to receive your point of view.

References

History of Options Trading. Retrieved from www.optiontradingpedia.com/history_of_options_trading.htm on 27th April 2020.

What Are Options Contracts? *Binance*, 3rd June 2019. Retrieved from www.binance.vision/economics/what-are-options-contracts%3famp=1

What is an Option? Retrieved from www.optionseducation.org/optionsoverview/what-is-an-option on 27th April 2020.

James Chen. "Expiration Date (Derivatives)." *Investopedia*, 9th Septemeber 2019.

James Chen. "Options." *Investopedia*, 19th February 2020.

James Chen. "Derivative." *Investopedia*, 27th January 2020.

Ron Ianieri. "The 4 Advantages of Options." *Investopedia*, 25th June 2019.

Nathan Reiff. "Hedge." *Investopedia*, 1st February 2020.

Jeff Kohler. "Implied Volatility: Buy Low and Sell High." *Investopedia*, 24th March 2020.

Chris B. Murphy. "Call Ratio Backspread Definition." *Investopedia*, 13th April 2019.

Will Kenton. "Put Ratio Backspread." *Investopedia*, 30th April 2018.

Brian Beers. "How the News Affects Stock Prices." *Investopedia*. 9th January 2020.

Manish Sahajwani. "10 Traits of a Successful Options Trader." *Investopedia*, 25th June 2019.

"Options Trading Styles." Retrieved from www.optionstradingpedia.com on 13th May 2020.

Troy Segal. "Fundamental Analysis." *Investopedia*, 16th March 2020.

Sean Vosler. *7 Figure Marketing Copy*. E-book.

Theresa W. Carey. "Best Options Trading Platforms." *Investopedia*, 1st May 2020.

Blain Reinkensmeyer. "Best Options Trading Platforms for 2020." *Stockbrokers.com*, 29th April 2020.

www.ingramcontent.com/pod-product-compliance
Lightning Source LLC
Chambersburg PA
CBHW052358220526
45465CB00003BB/1153